Thank You for Purchasing

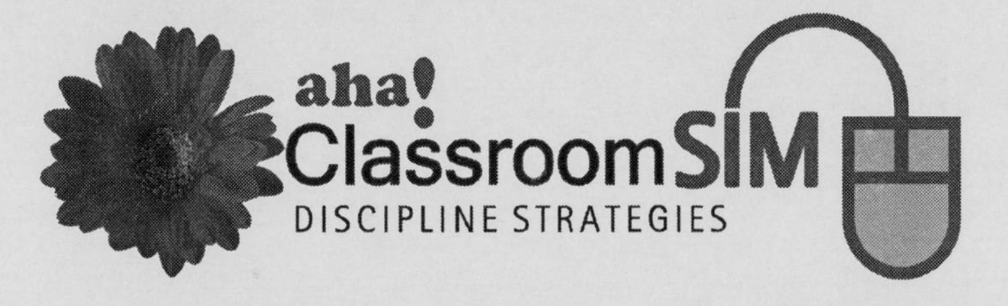

A 21st Century Teacher Training Tool

Your Activation Code:

9417e1f137847035fcfd

INSTALLATION INSTRUCTIONS

1. On the Internet, go to the aha! Process online store at www.ahaprocess.com/store/sim/
2. Download the SIM application—choosing grade level and computer platform
3. Install the Simulation

   PC version: Open and run the "setup.exe" file you downloaded

   Mac version: Expand the setup file with StuffIt® Expander
4. Follow the directions on the screen
5. Open the "Classroom Sim" application
6. Select the "activate" button and then enter your email address and the activation code provided above. Your computer needs to be connected to the internet during the activation process.

   (If you choose not to activate the Sim you will still be able to run the simulation in demo mode which provides limited access.)

COMPUTER REQUIREMENTS

PC VERSION	MAC VERSION
Windows 98/2000/XP	MAC OS 10.4
500 MHz processor	256 MB RAM
256 MB RAM	

aha! Classroom Sim™
Interactive Teacher Training Tool *for* Improving Classroom Discipline Skills

Who will be part of your classroom?

- **Students** with individual profiles **and their parents**
- **Administrators** (over the intercom)
- **School district** personnel (through student handbooks and other district-wide procedures)
- **Others** (through telephone calls and knocks on the door)

What you will encounter in the Classroom Sim?

- Events, behaviors, and interactions that take place in typical **classrooms**
- Discipline issues you must **prepare for and respond to** in your classroom
- Opportunities to **assess the effectiveness of your rules** and procedures and modify them as needed.

When do you receive feedback?

At the end of each simulated quarter you will receive a score showing how your decisions affected the **happiness**, **behavior**, and **academic** performance of your class.

This simulation was designed as a companion to the book, *Working with Students: Discipline Strategies for the 21st Century Classroom*, by Dr. Ruby Payne.

To be successful, you will need to effectively manage discipline issues originating both inside and outside of your classroom so that your students learn as much as possible. Ultimately, students in a well-disciplined classroom will learn more and be happier. We hope you enjoy your Classroom Sim. Have a great school year!

Sincerely,

Ruby K. Payne and the aha! Process Team

WORKING WITH STUDENTS

Discipline Strategies for the Classroom

Ruby K. Payne, Ph.D.
Working with Students: Discipline Strategies for the Classroom
142 pp.
ISBN-13: 978-1-92922-968-0
ISBN-10: 1-92922-968-2

1. Education 2. Sociology 3. Title

Published by **aha!** Process, Inc.

Copy editing by Dan Shenk
Book design by Paula Nicolella
Cover design by Dunn+ Design

NOTE: Some of the questions used in this book also were used in a Kappa Delta Phi/**aha!** Process study on how expert teachers respond to classroom situations.

WORKING WITH STUDENTS

Discipline Strategies for the Classroom

Ruby K. Payne, Ph.D.

TABLE OF CONTENTS

- *Where do you draw the line between personal and professional involvement with students?*
- *How do you handle a frantic student whose parent requires him/her to get straight A's?*

Procedures Checklist: Grades 9–12

CHAPTER ONE

SIX BASIC COMPONENTS OF CLASSROOM DISCIPLINE AND MANAGEMENT

1 CLASSROOMS ARE SYSTEMS

Classrooms are systems. If you want to have good discipline, then you must think of your classroom as a system, and you must manage it as a system.

Think of your classroom as a highway system with stoplights, intersecting roads, rules about turning, staying in the proper lane, etc. If we didn't have a system for highways and roads, driving would be impossible—or at least impossibly dangerous. Even when you know the system for driving and highways, you still have to watch each driver. But without a system, it would be total chaos. So your classroom must have a system.

Therefore, *within your classroom,* your system would do well to include the following:

	ON THE HIGHWAY	IN YOUR CLASSROOM
PROCEDURES	Which lane you are in, who goes first at a stop sign, etc.	How do students pass out papers? How do students put materials away?
RULES	When you stop and go, who has the right of way, etc.	What happens if a student cheats? If a cell phone rings during class? If a student curses? Etc.
MOTIVATION (consequences and rewards)	What motivates me to drive well? Example: Tickets, lower insurance rates for good driving, jail, etc.	What would motivate students to learn and behave?
ORGANIZATION AND PLANNING	Which is the best route to use? What do I need to take?	When are assignments due? How do students control impulsivity?
SCHEDULES	When do I need to leave to get there on time? Where do I need to go today?	What time does this subject or class start? What will happen next? When do students go to the next center or class?
PARTICIPANTS	Other drivers: How do all the drivers travel safely in the same space?	Students: How does a group of students work together safely and productively?
PERSON IN CHARGE	My driving: Am I aggressive, engaged in road rage, distracted by my cell phone?	Teacher: What is my approach to students when I discipline them?

Many beginning teachers don't address the classroom as a system. That would be like driving without knowing most of the pieces listed above. Use the checklist as a tool to know *your own* system.

2 THE LARGER SYSTEM—YOUR CAMPUS

Once you know the system for your classroom, you have to figure out how it works within the larger system of your campus. To continue the highway analogy, what happens if people repeatedly speed when they drive? They are taken out of the highway system and addressed by the much larger law enforcement/legal/judicial system. Sometimes students need to be taken out of the classroom system and addressed by the administration. So what are the components of the larger system?

1. The principal and/or assistant principal
2. The support staff (counselors, social workers, nurses, et al.)
3. Backup system of consequences and rewards (detention, school-sponsored parties, etc.)
4. District support system (alternative schools, student advocates, etc.)
5. Policies about suspension, expulsion, etc.

If you are a beginning teacher, here are questions you need to get answered before school starts:

1. What is the principal's approach to discipline?
2. Who are the support staff persons available and what are their roles?
3. What larger backup systems are available to individual teachers? For example: school-sponsored detention, Saturday school, timeout room, etc.
4. Does the district have a backup system for removing students from the school?
5. For which behaviors are students suspended? Expelled?

3 INDIVIDUAL STUDENTS

Ninety percent of your discipline referrals will come from 10% of your students. Skilled teachers identify these students within the first week of school. Students take on roles that determine many interactions within the classroom. To be sure, students can and do change, but certain behavioral patterns tend to emerge nonetheless. (See following chart with roles in the classroom.) These roles give each class a "personality." Some classes are much easier than others. Once skilled teachers identify the roles that students are playing in the classroom, they set up systems to help "manage" those roles. Sometimes a class will have a "critical mass" of difficult students. This will require an even more sophisticated and finely tuned systemic approach.

In the highway analogy, what happens when the individual driver repeatedly endangers others? When there's a pattern of recklessness? When the individual drives drunk? How do you address individuals within the dynamics of the classroom?

Student Roles in the Classroom

TYPE	WANTS	INTERVENTIONS
Perfectionist	To be perfect	Make sure they have all the details. Provide a rubric for evaluation.
Bully	To be in control	Identify the parameters of behaviors acceptable in your classroom. This student will not respect you unless you are personally strong.
Silent	To be invisible	Call on the student. Set up academic tasks so the student must interact with someone.

Student Roles in the Classroom *(continued)*

TYPE	WANTS	INTERVENTIONS
Entertainer	To ease discomfort, provide fun	Provide opportunities with academic tasks for humor. Show the student you have a sense of humor about yourself.
Social connector	To be friends	Provide opportunity for him/her to talk while doing academic work.
Social isolate	* Varies by individual	Assign paired activities, which necessitate a social interaction. Outline the parameters of the behaviors of the classroom.
Arguer	To be right	Let the student have the last word but not the last 10 sentences. Build an opportunity to argue into academic tasks.
Leader	To take charge	Build opportunities for leadership into the classroom.
Instigator	To be in control	Clearly outline what will and will not be acceptable in your classroom. Have clear consequences. Build a relationship of mutual respect with this student.
Distracter	To not be held accountable academically	Identify the source of the problem. Can he/she read?
Special needs	* Varies by individual; may have biochemical or neurological basis	Identify the need.

Source: Ruby K. Payne, *A Framework for Understanding Poverty Trainer Certification Manual*

INVOLVING PARENTS

Another part of discipline is the role of students' parents/guardians and your interactions with them. Should you involve them every time—or only some of the time? How do you determine when to involve them and to what extent? For what reasons?

To continue the highway analogy, what happens when the lawyers get involved and advocate for their client? Or what happens when the client does not have a lawyer? Who advocates for them? How does that change the dynamics? So it is with the classroom; the same questions apply to students and their parents. To state it even more simply: When and how do you involve parents?

Basically, parents tend to fall into one of five groups:

- Overprotective
- Hands-off approach
- Concerned and appropriate
- Unavailable
- Caring but unable to help

So the approach you use will depend at least in part on the parent.

Parents have varying degrees of skills and understandings about students, children, and child development. It's important to note that most teachers have much more exposure to children and adolescents than most parents do. So the understandings that teachers have about student behaviors are often better developed and more research-based than many parents have. But most parents have a very deep emotional bond to the student (their child!) that the teacher doesn't have. Even if they don't "parent" their child as you wish they would, they love their children and will defend them.

How you approach parents will make a big difference. (See the following planning worksheet.) If you are a beginning teacher, it helps to complete this worksheet. Know what you want to accomplish before you have the phone conference or visit in person.

PARENT/TEACHER CONFERENCE FORM WITH STUDENT

Student name _________________ Date__________ Time__________

Parent name__________________ Teacher______________________

PURPOSE OF CONFERENCE (CHECK AS MANY AS APPLY)

________ scheduled teacher/parent conference
________ student achievement issue
________ parent-initiated
________ discipline issue
________ social/emotional issue

WHAT IS THE DESIRED GOAL OF THE CONFERENCE?

WHAT DATA WILL I OR THE STUDENT SHOW THE PARENT?
Student work, discipline referrals, student planning documents?

WHAT QUESTIONS NEED TO BE ASKED? WHAT ISSUES NEED TO BE DISCUSSED?

WHAT FOLLOW-UP TOOLS AND STRATEGIES WILL BE IDENTIFIED?

Source: Ruby K. Payne, *No Child Left Behind Series: Parent and Community Involvement, Part IV*

5 TEACHER'S APPROACH TO DISCIPLINE

Three basic beliefs about discipline tend to be used among teachers.

- Some believe that behavior is caused by the thinking and so use a more cognitive approach.
- Some believe behavior is developmental and so use a teaching/learning approach.
- Some believe behavior is strictly a learned response to prior stimuli.

Most teachers have a mix of beliefs and use a combined approach. In the research on styles of discipline, three are generally cited: authoritarian, permissive, and negotiated. Most skilled teachers use a combination—depending on the situation, the student, and the safety considerations.

The research on "voices" done by Eric Berne is particularly helpful. (See Appendix, page 138.) The voice the teacher starts out with usually determines the outcome of an incident. (Following is a worksheet on page 10 a teacher can use with students to stay in the adult voice.) The ***child*** voice tends to be when a person is whining. The ***parent*** voice is a "telling" or "ordering" voice. There is a positive version (calm but insistent—example: "You must be seated now") and a negative version (when you have your index finger up and are giving a "should not" or "ought not to" lecture). The ***adult*** voice is when you're asking questions for understanding. Research indicates that 80% of discipline referrals come from 11% of the teachers (which is the other side of the coin from the earlier-cited statistic that 90% of discipline referrals come from 10% of the students). One of the big reasons for the high number of referrals by a relatively small number of teachers is the tendency of many of those teachers to use the negative parent voice, which doesn't really help in changing student behavior.

The best approach is usually one in which the teacher starts out in the adult voice and finishes in the positive parent voice with a consequence. Examples:

- Adult voice—"Help me understand where you were for 25 minutes …"
- Positive parent voice—"I'm sorry you chose to be lost for 25 minutes. Because of that choice, you also have chosen two hours in detention."

Most importantly, skilled teachers understand that when there is mutual respect in the classroom, discipline referrals drop. To quote Grant East, "Rules without relationships breed rebellion." For the classroom to be successful, there must be an atmosphere of mutual respect. (See "Do You Do These Things?" on page 11 and "Rubric for Mutual Respect" on page 12.)

You, the teacher, have the final responsibility for what happens in your classroom. For classrooms to work there has to be a final authority. That is you, the teacher. If that role is abdicated, the classroom degenerates into chaos.

How do you build relationships of mutual respect?

Students look for—and need—three things:

- Insistence
- Support
- High expectations (not unreasonable, but high)

Worksheet for student to use to stay in adult voice:

NAME:

1. What did you do? ______________________________
2. When you did that, what did you want? ______________________________
3. List four other things you could have done.

    1) ______________________________

    2) ______________________________

    3) ______________________________

    4) ______________________________

4. What will you do next time? ______________________________

Source: Ruby K. Payne, *A Framework for Understanding Poverty*

Do You Do These Things?

Please rate on a scale of 1 to 4 (with 4 being the highest).

Issue	**1**	**2**	**3**	**4**
Teacher calls students by name.				
Teacher uses courtesies: "please," "thank you," etc.				
Students use courtesies with each other and with teacher.				
Teacher calls on all students.				
Teacher gets into proximity (within arm's reach) of all students—daily if possible, but at least weekly.				
Teacher gives wait time for answers.				
Teacher smiles at students.				
Classroom has businesslike atmosphere.				
Student work/awards are displayed.				
Student bathrooms are clean.				
Grading/scoring is clear and easily understood.				
Students may ask for help from teacher.				
Teacher gives students specific reasons for praise.				

Adapted from TESA (Teacher Expectations & Student Achievement), Los Angeles Department of Education

Rubric for Mutual Respect

Issue	Evidenced	Needed	Not Applicable
Teacher calls students by name.			
Teacher uses courtesies: "please," "thank you," etc.			
Students use courtesies with each other and with teacher.			
Teacher calls on all students.			
Teacher gets into proximity (within an arm's reach) of all students—daily if possible, but at least weekly.			
Teacher greets students at door.			
Teacher smiles at students.			
Classroom has businesslike atmosphere.			
Students are given tools to assess/evaluate own work.			
Student-generated questions are used as part of instruction.			
Grading/scoring is clear and easily understood.			
Students may ask for extra help from teacher.			

Source: Ruby K. Payne, "Rubric for Mutual Respect"

ADDRESSING PARTICULAR INDIVIDUAL BEHAVIORS

Last, but not least, are the strategies for dealing with individual behaviors. Just as law enforcement has specific techniques for stopping a car, asking for a license, getting proof of insurance, etc., so you as the teacher need specific techniques for addressing particular behaviors.

Deciding if a particular behavior is actually a problem requires these questions:

1. Is this behavior endangering the student or other students?
2. Is this behavior interfering with teaching or learning?

If the answer to either of these questions is yes, then a discipline intervention needs to be identified and used.

Procedures Checklist

The following checklist is adapted from Guidelines for the First Days of School, from the Research Development Center for Teacher Education, Research on Classrooms, University of Texas, Austin.

STARTING CLASS	MY PROCEDURE
Taking attendance	
Marking absences	
Tardy students	
Giving makeup work for absentees	
Enrolling new students	
Un-enrolling students	
Students who have to leave school early	
Warm-up activity (that students begin as soon as they walk into classroom)	

INSTRUCTIONAL TIME	MY PROCEDURE
Student movement within classroom	
Use of cell phones and headphones	
Student movement in and out of classroom	
Going to restroom	
Getting students' attention	
Students talking during class	
What students do when their work is completed	
Working together as group(s)	
Handing in papers/homework	
Appropriate headings for papers	

INSTRUCTIONAL TIME	MY PROCEDURE
Bringing/distributing/using textbooks	
Leaving room for special class	
Students who don't have paper and/or pencils	
Signal(s) for getting student attention	
Touching other students in classroom	
Eating food in classroom	
Laboratory procedures (materials and supplies, safety routines, cleaning up)	
Students who get sick during class	
Using pencil sharpener	
Listing assignments/homework/ due dates	
Systematically monitoring student learning during instruction	

ENDING CLASS	MY PROCEDURE
Putting things away	
Dismissing class	
Collecting papers and assignments	

OTHER	MY PROCEDURE
Lining up for lunch/recess/special events	
Walking to lunch/recess	
Putting away coats and backpacks	
Cleaning out locker	
Preparing for fire drills and/or bomb threats	
Going to gym for assemblies/pep rallies	
Respecting teacher's desk and storage areas	
Appropriately handling/using computers/equipment	

STUDENT ACCOUNTABILITY	MY PROCEDURE
Late work	
Missing work	
Extra credit	
Redoing work and/or retaking tests	
Incomplete work	
Neatness	
Papers with no names	
Using pens, pencils, colored markers	
Using computer-generated products	
Internet access on computers	
Setting and assigning due dates	
Writing on back of paper	
Makeup work and amount of time for makeup work	

STUDENT ACCOUNTABILITY	MY PROCEDURE
Letting students know assignments missed during absence	
Percentage of grade for major tests, homework, etc.	
Explaining your grading policy	
Letting new students know your procedures	
Having contact with all students at least once during week	
Exchanging papers	
Using Internet for posting assignments and sending them in	

HOW WILL YOU ...	MY PLAN
Determine grades on report cards (components and weights of those components)?	
Grade daily assignments?	
Record grades so that assignments and dates are included?	
Have students keep records of their own grades?	
Make sure your assignments and grading reflect progress against standards?	
Notify parents when students are not passing or having other academic problems?	
Contact parents if problem arises regarding student behavior?	
Contact parents with positive feedback about their child?	
Keep records and documentation of student behavior?	
Document adherence to IEP (individualized education plan)?	
Return graded papers in timely manner?	
Monitor students who have serious health issues (peanut allergies, diabetes, epilepsy, etc.)?	

CHAPTER TWO

DISCIPLINE STRATEGIES: KINDERGARTEN–GRADE 2

In kindergarten through second grade, most children respond favorably to rewards and incentives that recognize appropriate, positive behavior.

Rewards can include a 15-minute party for good overall classroom behavior, individual stickers, paper money, points, and stars. Consequences can include charts, "stoplights," colored cards, and names on the board.

Many teachers establish in-class rules and have the students themselves, in cooperation with the teacher, come up with rules that would help them learn.

What do you do when a child hits or bites another child?

STEPS	ACTION
1.	Immediately separate the hitter or biter from the child he/she hit or bit.
2.	Try to determine the cause by asking this question: "What did you want or need when you did that?"
3.	Ask yourself, "Is this a habitual pattern or a one-time situation?"
4.	If habitual, go to Step 6. If one-time, find out the cause and enforce a timeout.
5.	With biting, inform both the administrator and the parents due to the risk of disease transmission.
6.	If the behavior is habitual, try these strategies: (a) Use a storybook approach (see *The Bear Who Did Not Know What to Do* on page 26); (b) give the student a stuffed animal to carry or hold; (c) give the student a squeezy ball to hold and squeeze, thereby releasing tension; (d) give the student colored markers or pencils and have him/her cartoon what happened, with two different endings—one ending what happened and the other what *could* have happened; (e) refer to a counselor or support staff; (f) use a metaphor story (see page 30); (g) use a smiley-face chart to have the student monitor his/her own behavior; and (h) require a pit stop on the racetrack (see racetrack technique on page 31).
7.	*Always document in writing the behavior/incident.*

What do you do when a child wants to touch everything and everyone?

Touching is a natural impulse, and it's particularly important for boys to have many opportunities to touch appropriately. Touching is a learning tool. What has to be identified is what may and may not be touched. Boys in particular show affection through their touches, hits, etc. So how do you provide those positive opportunities in the classroom?

	STRATEGIES
1.	Teach the whole class a lesson about touching at school. Go over what to touch and what not to touch.
2.	When students are walking in a line, have them interlock their hands/fingers behind their backs.
3.	Have a few stuffed animals available in the classroom that the students can touch or hold.
4.	Identify *not touching* as a positive behavior that allows your car to move on the racetrack.
5.	Teach the concept of personal space, which is one arm's length from another person.

How do you handle students who cannot stay in their seats?

In kindergarten, this would be handled differently from second grade. Here are some strategies.

	STRATEGIES
1.	Have the student stand in front of you and bend slightly. Wave your hand behind them and tell them you are putting glue on their seat, and when they sit down the glue will hold them there.
2.	Give positive reinforcements for staying in the seat.
3.	Teach how to move without bothering other students.
4.	Give students clipboards so they can work in more than one space.
5.	Teach lessons through music and movement.
6.	Have students stand and bend between activities.

How do you handle a constant talker?

	STRATEGIES
1.	Put bulletin board paper on desks and have a no-talking time when the only way students can communicate is to write to each other on the paper.
2.	Teacher proximity
3.	Move the student.
4.	Have a designated time to talk.
5.	Have students work together and talk to each other while they work. Give them a step sheet to check off tasks as they finish them.
6.	Have the constant talker be the "shusher." Shushers put their fingers to their mouths to quiet the group.
7.	Have them speak into a tape recorder—read a story, make an announcement, read the news, etc.

What planning tools do you give students to manage their own behavior?

STEPS	ACTION
1.	Give students stopwatches that they set, and have a given amount of time to get something done.
2.	Use the racetrack approach and help them plan how to get to the finish line by the end of the day.
3.	Place or draw three pictures on a sheet of paper. Each picture represents a learning center. As the student does that learning center, he/she puts an X on that picture. When all three pictures are X'd, the student gives it to the teacher and gets a sticker.
4.	Use the stellar behavior self-assessment.

How do you help students make appropriate decisions about routines?

One of the easiest ways is to use the storybook approach with students. *The Bear Who Did Not Know What to Do* is an example of the storybook approach that involves classroom participation.

STEPS	ACTION
1.	Read the story of the bear who didn't know what to do.
2.	Put example cartoons on the wall by each learning station or routine (example attached).
3.	Discuss self-talk. What do you say to yourself when you don't know what to do? Identify these three options for the students: "Watch other students, watch the teacher, look at the direction pictures."

THE BEAR WHO DID NOT KNOW WHAT TO DO

Once upon a time there was a bear who did not know what to do. He had never been to school. So when he got on the bus, the first thing he did was sit on the bus driver's lap.

What should he have done?

We sit down in our own seat.

Then he got to school, and he ran into the classroom, jumped on a desk, and said, "I am here!"

What should he have done?

Then he saw a new bear, and he ran up to him and knocked him down and said, "HI!"

What should he have done?

We are polite to others.

Then he saw the teacher bear and yelled at the teacher bear.
She said, "Please sit down."
He said, "I will not."

What should he have done?

Then he saw another bear who had a toy he wanted. So he ran up to him and took the toy away.

What should he have done?

Classmates share toys.

And when it was time to go to lunch, he sat and on the floor and cried.

What should he have done?

(Teachers can make up as many different scenarios as they wish. It's a participatory way for students to identify the correct behavior. Read the story many times. Students like the repetition, and it can be an effective teaching tool for behavior.)

STORYBOOK TECHNIQUE

This is a mental model for use with young children to help them identify the appropriate behaviors.

1. Get a blank book.
2. Identify, using stick figures, the student you are working with—e.g., This is you, Robert.
3. Identify his/her feelings when he/she did the behavior—e.g., Robert is mad.
4. Identify what the student actually did—e.g., Robert kicked the teacher.
5. Identify how the victim felt—e.g., Teacher is hurt. Teacher cried.
6. Identify what the student could have said—e.g., I am angry because …
7. Identify what the student's body should do—e.g., Feet should be on the floor.
8. Identify how the student will feel if he/she is doing the behavior correctly—e.g., Robert is calm.
9. Identify how the victim will feel if the student is doing the behavior correctly—e.g., Teacher is calm.

Then have the student read over the pictures until the student can tell the story from the pictures. When the student does the behavior, you give present the blank book and tell him/her to read it until he/she can behave appropriately. If the behavior is not in the book, someone (principal, counselor) draws it in the book and makes sure the student can tell it from the pictures before he/she leaves the office.

Robert
feeling
Robert
angry
mad
did
kicked teacher
victim
felt
hurt the
teacher
words
I am
mad
body
feet on
floor
feel
Robert
calm
victim
feel
teacher
calm

USING METAPHOR STORIES

Another technique for working with students and adults is to use a metaphor story. A metaphor story will help a student give voice to issues that affect subsequent actions. A metaphor story doesn't have any proper names in it and might go like this:

A student keeps going to the nurse's office two or three times a week. There is nothing wrong with her. Yet she keeps going. An adult says to Jennifer, the girl, "Jennifer, I am going to tell a story and I need you to help me. It's about a fourth-grade girl much like you. I need you to help me tell the story because I'm not in fourth grade.

"Once upon a time there was a girl who went to the nurse's office. Why did the girl go to the nurse's office? *(Because she thought there was something wrong with her.)* So the girl went to the nurse's office because she thought there was something wrong with her. Did the nurse find anything wrong with her? *(No, the nurse did not.)* So the nurse did not find anything wrong with her, yet the girl kept going to the nurse. Why did the girl keep going to the nurse? *(Because she thought there was something wrong with her.)* So the girl thought something was wrong with her. Why did the girl think there was something wrong with her? *(She saw a TV show ...)"*

The story continues until the reason for the behavior is found, whatever it may be, and then the story needs to end on a positive note. "So she went to the doctor, and he gave her tests and found that she was OK."

This is an actual case. What came out in the story was that Jennifer had seen a TV show in which a girl her age had died suddenly and had never known she was ill. Jennifer's parents took her to the doctor, he ran tests, and he told her she was fine. So she didn't go to the nurse's office anymore.

A metaphor story is to be used one on one when there's a need to understand the existing behavior and motivate the student to implement the appropriate behavior.

Adapted from Ruby K. Payne, *A Framework for Understanding Poverty*

RACETRACK TECHNIQUE

1. Make one wall of your room a racetrack. Give each student a car with a number on it.
2. Make a grid on the wall of the Daytona 500. Each car is on the list. Each time they cross the finish line, a tally mark is put by the car.
3. Make a list of "good behaviors" on the wall; the behaviors are "how to get your car to move." Emphasize with the students that the behaviors must be done all of the time so that the teacher can see when you do them.
4. When students have a bad day, they have a flat tire. They have to park their car by the road. Make a list of things to do to get your tire fixed. These again are good behaviors.
5. Occasionally a student will have a very bad day, and the transmission falls out. The student will have to go into the pit to get it fixed. But there is a list of behaviors to get your transmission fixed so you can get back on the road.

Add-on systems

1. planning
2. ***for***–toward (future story)

Each student has a car with a number on it.

STELLAR BEHAVIOR SELF-ASSESSMENT

The Five Points of Stellar Behavior

The word *stellar* means starlike.

There are **five points** of stellar behavior.

- The **first point** is your right arm. If you remembered to raise your hand before speaking out, shade in or color the right "arm" of your star. If you did not, try again tomorrow.

- The **second point** is your left arm. If you used your hands to help rather than to hurt other people, shade in or color the left arm of your star. If you did not, try again tomorrow.

- The **third point** is your right leg. If you walked rather than ran, inside the building, shade in or color the right "leg" of your star. If you did not, you can try again tomorrow.

- The **fourth point** is your left leg. If you walked only to the place that you needed and had permission to be, shade in or color the left leg of your star. If you did not, you try again tomorrow.

- The **fifth and most important point** is your mind. If you worked to develop your mind in a positive way, shade in or color the "head" of your star. If you did not, try again tomorrow.

- Each of the five points affects the kind of person you are becoming in your heart. If you were able to shade in or color all five of the points of your star, then shade in or color the "heart" of your star. If you were not able to color the heart of your star today, try again tomorrow.

Now you are on your own. At the end of each day assess your own behavior and shade or fill in each part of the star that you have earned. At the end of the month look over your stars and determine where you are doing well and where you need to concentrate your efforts toward stellar behavior.

Month: ______________________________

Sunday	Monday	Tuesday	Wednesday	Thursday	Friday	Saturday
☆	☆	☆	☆	☆	☆	☆
Date____	____	____	____	____	____	____
☆	☆	☆	☆	☆	☆	☆
Date____	____	____	____	____	____	____
☆	☆	☆	☆	☆	☆	☆
Date____	____	____	____	____	____	____
☆	☆	☆	☆	☆	☆	☆
Date____	____	____	____	____	____	____
☆	☆	☆	☆	☆	☆	☆
Date____	____	____	____	____	____	____

This month my behavior was ______________________________

______________________________.

Next month I plan to ______________________________

______________________________.

Source: Bethanie H. Tucker, "Stellar Behavior Self-Assessment"

PROCEDURES CHECKLIST: K–2

The following checklist for K–2 has been adapted from Guidelines for the First Days of School from the Research Development Center for Teacher Education, Research on Classrooms, University of Texas, Austin.

Cissy Longoria, Corpus Christi, Texas, prepared this sample checklist.

STARTING CLASS	MY PROCEDURE
Taking attendance	Each morning as students arrive, absences and tardies are recorded in a folder the office provides. The folder is placed outside the door for someone from the office to pick up.
Marking absences	In addition, the teacher records absences in his/her gradebook. A = absent; TE = tardy excused; TU = tardy unexcused.
Tardy students	If a student is late, the teacher asks the student to go back to the office and get a *tardy slip*. The office will sign the permit and code the tardy. The teacher then records that in the office folder and in the gradebook.
Giving makeup work for absentees	A student is assigned to collect all work given for the day. The teacher then gives all missed work to the child who was absent. Work can either be made up at home or in class if time allows.
Enrolling new students	The office enrolls new students. Children are assigned to the teacher in each grade level. The assignment depends upon if the child is bilingual and/or how many children the teacher already has. Example: The teacher with the lowest count will get the new child.

STARTING CLASS	MY PROCEDURE
Un-enrolling students	The teacher fills out a dismissal form that the office provides. The form will include a place for grades and levels of math and reading. The teacher averages the grades from the gradebook and provides the completed copy for the office. Cumulative folders on the child also must be completed. The teacher's signature, days present, and days absent also will be provided on both the withdrawal form and the cumulative folder. All personal supplies and folders are given to the child to take along. Any library or cafeteria dues must be cleared before the student is withdrawn and cleared.
Students who have to leave school early	The office lets the teacher know by intercom that a child needs to go to the office because he/she is leaving for the day. The teacher then instructs the child to get his/her homework folder and backpack and walk quietly to the office. The child then walks to the office escorted by a responsible peer.
Warm-up activity (that students begin as soon as they walk into classroom)	Students come in and start writing in their "My Journal" spirals. They are allowed to write about anything they like. Sharing of journals is usually done on the carpet during shared reading time.

INSTRUCTIONAL TIME	MY PROCEDURE
Student movement within classroom	Students must raise their hand to go to the restroom. Only assigned classroom monitors may be up to help the teacher. Students also are allowed to get up to go to computers to take an Accelerated Reading test. Once again, students must raise their hand to get up to test. All students also are allowed to go to designated learning stations throughout the day. Students are put into groups for literacy and math stations. Students rotate every 15–20 minutes.

INSTRUCTIONAL TIME	MY PROCEDURE
Use of cell phones and headphones	The teacher uses a cell phone for instant communication with the parents. Students may not use cell phones in the classroom. The teacher communicates both unacceptable behaviors and also positive behaviors to parents. Headphones are utilized during computer and listening/reading/phonic stations.
Student movement in and out of classroom	This classroom is self-contained. (This year I have no special education students who go to "resource." There is a marked effort not to identify first-graders for special education.) Students are allowed to go to the library throughout the day. Students are to go and check out library books. Students usually go to the library in pairs. The teacher escorts students to lunch, physical education, computer lab, and science lab at the designated times on the designated days.
Going to restroom	This classroom has a bathroom. Students are allowed to use it if they raise their hand and ask. The teacher also allows them to go without asking if they are sick or simply cannot wait. The students are allowed to enter the restroom when the red stop sign is turned to the green-colored sign.
Getting students' attention	One way to get students' attention is to ring a bell for students to rotate to another activity station. Another is to play the "I spy" game. This is where the teacher says, "I spy a person who is sitting up straight, listening, and not talking. This student is wearing ..." Students then get quiet and look around to figure out who I am talking about. Other times the teacher may simply stop talking until everyone is listening.

INSTRUCTIONAL TIME	**MY PROCEDURE**
Students talking during class	If students are talking, the teacher politely asks them to stop. If the teacher asks again, they have been warned. Each student has a "clothesline" and a clothespin on that line. The third time, the clothespin is moved from green (meaning good) to yellow (not so good). The next time, the clothespin is moved to red (not good at all). These clothespin colors are recorded and sent to parents on the *Behavior Chart* that is sent home daily.
What students do when their work is completed	Students may read books on their level and test for Accelerated Reader on one of the four computers that are in the classroom. They also are allowed to practice and review any needed skills. The students are able to use dry-erase boards, workbooks, etc. They also may check to see if they can edit, lengthen, or improve any writing they have been working on in their *Writers Workshop Folder*.
Working together as group(s)	Students work in cooperative groups for various subjects. Science lab work is always in a group. Groups are used to practice math and reading skills. Groups also are used to create projects for social studies, holidays, etc.
Handing in papers/homework	At the start of school, the teacher assigns each student a number. All papers and homework are handed in or packed up in order of their assigned numbers. Numbers also are listed in the same order in the gradebook. Student helpers pick up all work and homework in the same order each day. This system helps to make grading, recording grades, and filing faster for the teacher.

INSTRUCTIONAL TIME	MY PROCEDURE
Appropriate headings for papers	All the headings on papers are done on the upper-right-hand corner of the paper. Example: *#4 (assigned number)* *Juan Perez* *September 17, 2006* (By the end of the year, first-graders can write both their first and last names on their papers.)
Bringing/distributing/using textbooks	All textbooks are checked out to the teachers by the assistant principal. All textbooks are kept on shelves and placed where students can easily reach them when they're needed.
Leaving room for special class	When students do leave for a special class, the student is picked up by the specialist.
Students who don't have paper and/or pencils	Students who don't have supplies may borrow from a classmate. The teacher buys extra supplies at the beginning of the school year. Students are able to keep the supplies that the teacher provides for them. If the student continues to lose or destroy supplies, the teacher calls the parent and explains the situation and asks for supplies to be brought to school.
Signal(s) for getting student attention	Without speaking, the teacher raises his/her hand in the air and puts a finger to his/her lips. Students all help each other to get quiet. This also can be done for an individual child. The teacher taps quietly on the table and puts a finger to his/her lips.
Touching other students in classroom	The teacher may give a "high five" to the students when they have accomplished a set goal of some kind. Sometimes the teacher can give them a light tap on their shoulder when they are doing well or trying their best.

INSTRUCTIONAL TIME	MY PROCEDURE
Eating food in classroom	Snacks are sometimes provided if the lunch schedule is changed to a later time. Lunch is eaten in the classroom during Science Fair because the projects are set up in the cafeteria. Two parties are allowed during the year. Cupcakes and a drink (provided by the parent) are allowed for a child's birthday.
Laboratory procedures (materials and supplies, safety routines, cleaning up)	Students follow safety rules that they were taught during a science lab safety video. Each group in the science lab has a student who is the supply monitor, a cleanup monitor, and a leader. All students are trained to do their assigned science job while in the lab. Routines are discussed, and monitors are assigned before they begin the science lab.
Students who get sick during class	Students who get sick are immediately sent to the school nurse. The nurse then determines if he/she needs to call the parent and if the child needs to be picked up.
Using pencil sharpener	Students are not allowed to use pencil sharpeners during class time. All pencils are sharpened before and after school. Individual personal small sharpeners are encouraged just in case their pencil tip gets broken. They also have the option of taking a pencil from the "Sharpened Pencils" jar and placing their pencil in the "Needs Sharpening" jar.
Listing assignments/ homework/due dates	All homework assignments and project due dates are listed on the students' weekly homework sheet. Homework for Monday through Friday is placed in the student's *homework folder*. All upcoming events and important dates to remember also are included.
Systematically monitoring student learning during instruction	The teacher observes each student during instruction. When the teacher sees a child struggling with a particular skill, the teacher works with that student one on one or in a small group. The teacher reteaches in a different way.

ENDING CLASS	MY PROCEDURE
Putting things away	At the end of the day, students are responsible for putting away learning-station games, dry-erase boards, markers, magnetic letters, pointers, books, word cards, sentence strips, etc. Students also are responsible for turning off my two classroom lights, as well as the four computers in the classroom. Finally, students put chairs up on desks and pick up any big pieces of paper around them.
Dismissing class	Students are given their homework folders and are lined up in the following order: 1. Bus students (picked up by a paraprofessional) 2. Latchkey students 3. Daycare students 4. Fellow teacher's students Pick-up students: I walk these students to the front of the school and wait for a parent, guardian, et al., to pick up the students.
Collecting papers and assignments	Classroom helpers collect papers for me in numerical order. My helpers can tell me if a student's work isn't in by telling me what number or numbers may be missing. All collected papers are paper clipped and placed in my "Grade Me" basket.

OTHER	MY PROCEDURE
Lining up for lunch/recess/special events	I have my desks grouped together. Some desks are grouped in fours, some in sixes, and some in sevens. I usually line up my students by calling out the groups that are behaving the best. Example: "Group 1, line up, Group 2, etc." When I have more time, I will line up students by asking them a spelling word or maybe a quick math problem, etc.
Walking to lunch/recess	I walk the students to lunch. Paraprofessionals take over while I go to the teachers' lounge for a 30-minute lunch break. Paras also walk students to recess when students have finished their lunch.

OTHER	MY PROCEDURE
Putting away coats and backpacks	All coats, jackets, sweaters, and backpacks are placed behind the child on his/her chair.
Cleaning out locker	There are no lockers in our classroom.
Preparing for fire drills and/or bomb threats	Students know that when we hear the fire-drill bell they are to line up as quickly as possible. Last person out the door is to turn off the lights and close the door (this student has already practiced and has been assigned the job). This is a very responsible student!
Going to gym for assemblies/pep rallies	Students are to line up in a quiet, orderly manner. I then lead students to assemblies, pep rallies, etc. Students should have hands to themselves and be walking on the third tile (this helps them keep a straight line).
Respecting teacher's desk and storage areas	Students are not allowed to touch anything on my teacher desk. Yet they do know that they are able to make words for word-study stations on the front part of my magnetic desk. Magnetic letters are items students may touch. Students know which teacher storage items are off limits to them.
Appropriately handling/using computers/equipment	I, along with the librarian, have instructed the students how to handle and use computers, CD players, tape players, etc. Students also work on a computer program that helps them to learn and practice various skills having to do with computers and their usage.

STUDENT ACCOUNTABILITY	MY PROCEDURE
Late work	Late work can be completed in class or taken home for extra reinforcement.
Missing work	Any missing work must be completed before a student can go to recess. Recess is a privilege and must be earned!

STUDENT ACCOUNTABILITY	MY PROCEDURE
Extra credit	Extra points are often given for learning and writing extra spelling words or any extended writing (stories, etc.). Also, for sentence exercises, I will give 3–5 extra points for additional sentences that are written correctly (capital letters, punctuation, word-wall words, etc.).
Redoing work and/or retaking tests	If a student missed work or a test because of an absence, he/she is able to redo the work when he/she returns. Work is collected and saved for the student by an assigned peer. The work/tests are then placed on my desk.
Incomplete work	Work that is incomplete must be done before students can go to any learning stations. Students also are not allowed to check out new books—or test on the computer—until all work is complete. My students always try to complete all work given. They love the rotating learning stations and don't want to miss out on the competition that is involved in the AK testing. They like to compete against each other. They also like to see who can read the most books daily and who can pass the most tests.
Neatness	Neatness is important! If work is sloppy, I have students redo the work, or I may take off points. Students usually do their best because they don't like the idea of redoing a paper.
Papers with no names	Papers with no names are sometimes thrown out. Usually, if I know who the person is I will take off points. At the start of school, I simply remind them not to forget their names. Toward the end of school, however, I don't usually have these problems. Students not only remember their names, they also write their assigned numbers.

STUDENT ACCOUNTABILITY	**MY PROCEDURE**
Using pens, pencils, colored markers	Students aren't allowed to use pens. I allow only pencils. Markers may be used for coloring or projects. Yellow highlighters are encouraged. I like to train the kids to highlight directions or main-idea passages, etc. Although they're only first-graders, they seem to understand the importance of doing this.
Using computer-generated products	Students are able to practice spelling words, writing sentences, etc., on the computer. Students also are able to do research on the computer. They can print what they need for their folders. They also are able to print any awards they earn from a particular program.
Internet access on computers	Students are able to access educational programs such as: • Starfall.com • Scholastic.com • Brainfun.com • Mathbrain.com
Setting and assigning due dates	All due dates of projects, reports, etc., are placed in our schoolwide newsletter that is sent out each Friday. Reminders also are sent out in our first-grade weekly homework sheet that is sent home each Monday. I also send extra reminders to my classroom parents.
Writing on back of paper	I ask my students *not* to write on the back of their papers. We make a lot of booklets and display them on our outside bulletin board. Reading them when writing on the back makes their work hard to read.
Makeup work and amount of time for makeup work	Makeup work after an absence can be made up the next day—or sometime within the week if absences were excessive.

STUDENT ACCOUNTABILITY	**MY PROCEDURE**
Letting students know assignments missed during absence	I explain to the students the work they missed while they were absent. Makeup work can be done at school or after school during tutoring. Some work also can be completed at home.
Percentage of grade for major tests, homework, etc.	I don't give grades for homework. All other grades are weighted equally (reading, math, science, social studies). For language, I average spelling grades and the language grades to get an average for language.
Explaining your grading policy	Our grading policy is sent to students in our *Welcome Back* packet at the start of the school year. I also explain the grading policy at conferences with my parents.
Letting new students know your procedures	I explain important procedures to the new students and show them around the room. I also have the new student shadow another child in my room. The new students learn very quickly where and how everything is done.
Having contact with all students at least once during week	During small-group instructions, I meet with all of my struggling students on a daily basis. All other students meet with me once or twice a week. I also check student progress by doing a lot of one-on-one testing.
Exchanging papers	No exchanging of papers is permitted in my classroom.
Using Internet for posting assignments and sending them in	I do *not* use the Internet for posting assignments.

HOW WILL YOU …	MY PLAN
Determine grades on report cards (components and weights of those components)?	Minimum of six grades or more are recorded in the gradebook. These grades are added and divided by the number of grades to get an average for the report card.
Grade daily assignments?	Daily grades are often taken to check for understanding. I also take grades on assessment day (Fridays).
Record grades so that assignments and dates are included?	I divide my gradebook by subjects and six weeks. All assignments, tests, and dates are included. I also include their reading and math level at a particular six weeks' period.
Have students keep records of their own grades?	Students do *not* keep records of their own grades.
Make sure your assignments and grading reflect progress against standards?	The district has set the objectives by six-week intervals and weekly alignment. I follow the district and school pacing guidelines. If students are not "on level" during our benchmark testing, grades also will reflect that they aren't on the level they should be on.
Notify parents when students are not passing or having other academic problems?	Progress reports are sent the third week of each six-week reporting period. Parents are informed if their child is F (failing) or B (borderline). All subjects in danger are on the progress report. A parent signature is required and must be returned the following day. I then call parents and set up conferences. I explain their child's difficulties and show them strategies, etc., so the students also can get help at home.
Contact parents if problem arises regarding student behavior?	I call parents from my cell phone or from home. I also have to fill out an office referral depending on the behavior. I keep in close contact with all of the parents. Parents usually hear from me before the referral makes it home.

HOW WILL YOU ...	MY PLAN
Contact parents with positive feedback about their child?	Daily reports are sent to parents in the homework folder. I send a behavior chart where I often write positive comments. I also have been known to call parents in the evening or weekends to report positive behavior.
Keep records and documentation of student behavior?	I keep all behavior charts for documentation. “Behavior Charts” are sent back and forth every day and are collected each six weeks. I then keep the charts because parents have read and signed them. I also keep all office referrals in my gradebook.
Document adherence to IEP (individualized education plan)?	I document all modifications from IEPs in my gradebook and lesson plans. I keep IEP folders in the back of each lesson plan book.
Return graded papers in timely manner?	All graded papers are sent home each Wednesday. Parents expect these papers on this particular day.
Monitor students who have serious health issues (peanut allergies, diabetes, epilepsy, etc.)?	Using the “Emergency Card” filled out by parents, I am able to be informed of each child’s health issues. With the help of the school nurse, I monitor students with any particular health issues.

CHAPTER THREE

DISCIPLINE STRATEGIES: GRADES 3–5

In Grades 3–5, in addition to the systems issues mentioned, teachers use rewards and consequences. Rewards can include a 15-minute good-behavior party, stickers, paper money, points, and stars. Consequences can include charts, stoplights, colored cards, and names on the board.

Again, as with K–2, many teachers establish in-class rules and have students help come up with the guidelines that would assist in their learning.

What do you do when a student will not finish or hand in work?

1. Does the child have a disability?
2. Can the student read?
3. Can the student do the work?
4. What motivates the student?
5. Is this a time-management skill issue?
6. Does the student have planning tools?

The first question to ask yourself is if the student can do the work. If the student can do the work, then move on to the steps listed below.

STEPS	ACTION
1.	Give students a planning tool for finishing work. For example, draw four circles on the blackboard. Write in each circle one thing that must be done and handed in. Give each student a half sheet of paper with four circles copied onto the paper. The students write on their own papers what they must do and hand in. As they finish each "circle" and hand it in, the students cross it off.
2.	Use the racetrack system and list "getting your work done" as one way to get your car to move.
3.	Provide a step sheet for each task and have students check off the steps as they do them.
4.	Work with a partner to get the work done.
5.	Incorporate a time to work before or after school—or during lunch or recess.
6.	Call home. Give a warning. Have a parent/teacher conference.

What do you do when students say mean things to one another?

STEPS	ACTION
1.	Have a classroom discussion (class meeting) about what a real compliment is. Many students believe that a real compliment is something sarcastic or negative.
2.	Teach lessons on respect.
3.	Identify the norms and expectations of your classroom.
4.	Teach basic manners: "please," "thank you," "I'm sorry."

What planning tools do you give students?

STEPS	ACTION
1.	Give students a planner that is monitored by parents and teachers.
2.	Send home a weekly newsletter about the assignments for the week.
3.	Post your assignments online.
4.	Provide study guides for major tests.
5.	Provide 3×5 note cards.
6.	Use a system involving manila folders and envelopes for managing projects and papers.

How do you handle a bully?

Bullying is both a system issue and an individual issue. In organizational research, there is a phenomenon known as "isomorphism," which means that what happens at one level of the organization happens at least in some measure at all levels. So if you have student bullies, you also tend to have teacher bullies and administrator bullies. In most school systems, student bullying is a zero-tolerance activity.

STEPS	ACTION
1.	Identify the action or behavior that was unacceptable.
2.	Ask this question: "When you did that, what did you want or need?"
3.	Identify alternative behavior(s).
4.	Identify consequences.
5.	Refer the case to the administration.

How do you handle the instigator—the student who creates many of the problems?

It's important to understand how an instigator works. First of all, instigators love omissions, the part of the story that is not told. And the instigator almost always uses sexual innuendo and insult. This can be verbal or nonverbal. Nonverbal messages often are used because they allow the instigator to be "innocent." Instigators also use a divide-and-conquer strategy; in other words, I'll tell you one thing and tell the other person something else.

If you wish to identify who your campus instigators are, a simple tool is available. Give every teacher and administrator a disposable camera. When there's a fight, the staff members take pictures.

Students scatter almost immediately. But usually the instigators are watching the fight, and they're in most of the pictures of the fight. To end the behavior, the following steps often help.

STEPS	ACTION
1.	First, talk individually to the students. This is the key question: *"Were you there when they said/did that?"* Almost always they weren't present; it was reported back to them.
2.	Ask who told them. Typically they won't tell you—particularly if it's a school bully. So you can ask, *"Did you have a* ***vision****?"* At that point they often will tell you the student's name.
3.	Repeat Steps 1 and 2 with the next student. You tend to get the same name(s). This is your instigator.
4.	Put the instigator between the two individuals and ask them to each tell the other what the instigator told them. Very quickly they hear the omission.
5.	If you want to end the behavior of the instigator, the instigator must receive the same consequences as the individuals who got into trouble as a result of the instigation.

What do you do when a student cheats?

STEPS	ACTION
1.	Document the activity.
2.	Give a zero.
3.	Sometimes teachers will give a test or alternative activity to find out what learning has occurred.
4.	Determine the intervention based on the reason(s) for cheating.

ASK YOURSELF …

What is the "payoff" for cheating?

- A passing grade
- Reduced anxiety about tests
- Less pressure from parents

What management tools do you give students?

STEPS	ACTION
1.	Use a system involving manila folders and envelopes for managing projects and papers.
2.	Make a list of the things that students are to have in their desks. Have them draw on paper the organizational arrangement of the items in their desks. Laminate these and lay them on the desks. During the last five minutes of the day, the students put their books back into their desks, according to the maps they made. Anything that isn't on the map is taken home or thrown away.
3.	Use 3×5 cards and have students write on one side a calendar for the week to identify when things must be done. On the other side they make a list of what they need to do that day. Each day they make a new card with their "plan for the day."
4.	Use colored folders for different subjects.
5.	Provide homework folders for parental review.
6.	Use step sheets.

PROCEDURES CHECKLIST: GRADES 3–5

The following checklist for Grades 3–5 has been adapted from Guidelines for the First Days of School from the Research Development Center for Teacher Education, Research on Classrooms, University of Texas, Austin.

Judy Weber, Yorktown, Indiana, prepared this sample checklist.

STARTING CLASS	MY PROCEDURE
Taking attendance	• Student pictures are mounted on business-card-sized magnets. • A "Question of the Day" is posted at the front of the room. The Question of the Day is related to content from the previous day. A variety of graphic organizers is used as the format to answer the question. Examples: T chart, Venn Diagram. • As students enter the classroom, each student answers the question and places his/her picture in the appropriate location on the graphic organizer. • The teacher determines who is present with a glance at the Question of the Day or while briefly discussing the question and answer with the students. • A teacher or student records attendance on the school attendance slip. A student helper takes the slip to the office. • At the beginning of the school year, the teacher explains and models the procedure. Students practice the procedure and revisit it as needed throughout the year.
Marking absences	• After the morning bell rings, the teacher or a student looks at the Question of the Day board and marks absences on the attendance slip of students who have not answered the Question of the Day. A student helper takes the attendance slip to the office. • The teacher marks absences in the gradebook under attendance.

STARTING CLASS	MY PROCEDURE
Tardy students	• Students entering the room after the second bell (tardy bell) return to the office for a tardy slip. • Tardy slips are filed in the student's individual file folder. • The teacher highlights in yellow the date on the attendance page in the gradebook to provide a quick method for determining the number of times a student has been tardy.
Giving makeup work for absentees	• Missed work is collected in a file folder for the student. • As each assignment is provided to students, a copy is added to the makeup-work folder. • Assignments are numbered. The teacher or a student writes a brief explanation of the assignment on a teacher-created Missed Assignment sheet. The numbered assignments correspond with the numbered explanation. • Assignments are generally due the next day or later if more than one day is missed. Students and/or parents may request more time as needed. • If more than one student is absent, the Missed Assignment sheet is copied and stapled to each folder. • The student returns the entire folder and places it in the Missed Assignment basket the next day and checks his/her name off the Missed Assignment list.
Enrolling new students	• The school nurse or secretary escorts a new student to the room and introduces the student to the teacher. • The teacher introduces the student to the class and welcomes the student. • The teacher provides the student with a desk and time to put away any items brought to the classroom. • A student in the classroom volunteers to partner with the new student for the first week to assist as needed. • A three-ring binder with classroom procedures is given to the student.

STARTING CLASS	MY PROCEDURE
Enrolling new students *(continued)*	• The teacher explains the procedures and shows the student where each is located in the binder. • Students model the classroom procedures for the new student. • The new student is added to the gradebook.
Un-enrolling students	• The school checklist is completed, and grades are recorded on the cumulative record. The report card, school supplies, and books are sent to the office by the end of the day that the student withdraws.
Students who have to leave school early	• The parent contacts the school by note or phone call. • The note is filed in the individual student's folder. • The office calls the room when the parents arrive. • Students go to the office with assignments and backpack. • The parent signs the student out of the building by recording the name of the student, time leaving, and reason for the early departure.
Warm-up activity (that students begin as soon as they walk into classroom)	• Empty backpacks and hang up coats and backpacks in the hallway before entering the room. • Put completed work in the labeled container (math, reading, etc.). • Answer the Question of the Day. • Sharpen pencils. • When the bell rings have journal out and be in seat writing in journal or completing the Problem of the Day. Example: Journal—MWF; Problem of the Day—T, TH. • Students share journal writing or discuss the answer to the Problem of the Day in a community meeting starting 15 minutes after the bell rings. • A timer is set on the overhead projector for 15 minutes in order for students to be aware of the time to complete the task.

INSTRUCTIONAL TIME	MY PROCEDURE
Student movement within classroom	• At the beginning of the school year, set up the room with student movement patterns in mind. Think about areas that may become overcrowded and make changes. When school begins, notice problem areas and make further changes. • Students move around the room based on the classroom procedure for the subject or activity. The teacher identifies the procedure at the outset. If no procedure exists, the teacher may interact with the students to create one. Movement procedures are provided in written form. • Transitions are taught, modeled, and practiced to achieve smooth, efficient transitions that take minimal class time.
Use of cell phones and headphones	• Cell phones are not allowed in school. • Headphones are allowed only during special occasions, at recess, or when working at the computer. • Headphones brought to school must stay in backpacks. • When headphones are in the classroom without permission, the teacher holds them until the end of the day. If it happens again, the teacher keeps the headphones and calls parents.

Student movement in and out of classroom	• Students follow school procedures when leaving the classroom. Students are expected to walk quietly in an orderly manner.
	• When lining up, the students follow the lining-up procedure for the classroom.
	  o Students work together to clean up the community supplies holder and floor area around their individual desks.
	  o To show one is ready, sit down and put head on desk, with no talking.
	  o The first group to get ready to line up is first in line.

INSTRUCTIONAL TIME	MY PROCEDURE
Student movement in and out of classroom *(continued)*	o One seating group at a time quietly walks to the door when the teacher calls the group to line up. o If a student in the group runs or talks when lining up, the entire group goes back to their desks and puts heads down. • Repeat the process until all groups follow the procedure. • This procedure is taught, modeled, and practiced at the beginning of the school year and revisited as needed throughout the year.
Going to restroom	• Restroom breaks are a regular part of the school day. Examples: before school starts, before recess, before and after lunch. • To use the restroom at other times, the student raises his/her hand with the pointer finger up or asks the teacher. • The students are to use the restroom, wash hands, get a drink of water, and return to the classroom in five minutes or less.
Getting students' attention	• Turn off lights. • Ring chimes. • Strike a wooden percussion object. • Use timer on overhead. • Clap.
Students talking during class	• Soft music/soft talking • No music/no talking • If the pink lights (or party lights) are on in the room, the students may talk quietly. • Lessons are designed with time to process information in structured and unstructured formats. Examples: Talk to your neighbor, find an elbow partner, go into a group work, etc. • Students are asked to monitor their voices—using whisper voice, small talking voice, or playground voice. Example: Use your playground voice when practicing for the play.

INSTRUCTIONAL TIME	MY PROCEDURE
What students do when their work is completed	• A bulletin board of numbered activities is available for students as work is finished. Students must complete the activities in sequential order. Some activities require a product to complete. A table to hold supplies, along with labeled stacked bins to hold products, are located under the bulletin board. • Read. Students may read a library book or go to the library in the classroom when work is completed. The classroom library is limited to two students at a time. The library closes when more than two students are in the area. • Write. Students may write in their journal when work is completed. • Post a list of content-specific activities on the board or chart paper that students may choose as work is completed.
Working together as group(s)	• Students are taught and practice how to work together in groups. • Students in a group assess how well each member of the group worked and how well the entire group worked together. They also set goals to improve group collaboration. • When students work in groups, the teacher uses a signal to get student attention quickly. Example: "Ring and freeze" procedure. Ring a bell or strike a chime; students freeze, teacher gives instructions, students continue. • During work time, students are allowed to work together quietly as they decide is necessary. Exceptions would include when students are taking a test or when one student is preventing another student (or students) from learning.

INSTRUCTIONAL TIME	MY PROCEDURE
Handing in papers/homework	• Each subject has a labeled basket in the room. • As students place their assignments in the appropriate basket, they mark a check on an assignment chart—or one student is in charge of checking in all assignments on a checklist. Each student's name is marked on a checklist to show that the assignment is in the basket.
Appropriate headings for papers	• One bonus point is given for each component of the heading on each assignment completed, with up to 3 bonus points per assignment. • 1 point for the subject/title, 1 for the placement of the name, 1 for the correct date in the correct location. • In the beginning of the school year, each component is marked by a +1 beside each correct item, or the item is corrected on each paper. • A model is posted in the classroom.
Bringing/distributing/ using textbooks	• Textbooks are distributed to students on the first few days of school. • Each student picks up a book, writes his/her name and school year in the book, and gives the teacher the book number to record. • The process is repeated until all books are distributed.
Leaving room for special class	• For each student attending a special class, a picture of an analog clock is placed on his/her desk to illustrate how the clock will look when the student leaves the classroom. • A small card is taped beside the clock to lists the time and provide the student with a list of items to take to the special class.

INSTRUCTIONAL TIME	MY PROCEDURE
Students who don't have paper and/or pencils	• At the beginning of the school year, a list of school supplies is given to each family. Two sets of school supplies are requested. • The supplies are stored for the students. • Students are placed in groups with community supply holders. • One day a week pencils are added. Other supplies are added as needed. • Each classroom in the building provides supplies. • No supplies travel from classroom to classroom or home.
Signal(s) for getting student attention	• Hand up—palm out. When the teacher's hand goes up, each student raises his/her hand and stops talking. When every hand is up the room is quiet. Students are allowed to tap another student or say "shhh" (non-verbal) to assist. • Count to 3; hold up each finger as you count. Students are to be quiet and seated at the end of the count. • "Ring and freeze." Ring a bell or strike a chime; students freeze, teacher gives instructions, students continue.
Touching other students in classroom	• Students are taught to respect others' possessions and bodies. • It is disrespectful to keep touching someone if asked to stop. • Students persisting after being asked to stop are temporarily moved out of the group setting.
Eating food in classroom	• Students may eat food in the classroom during special occasions, such as parties or lessons that involve food. • As a rule, students do not bring food to school or into the classroom without permission.

INSTRUCTIONAL TIME	MY PROCEDURE
Laboratory procedures (materials and supplies, safety routines, cleaning up)	• Use a pocket chart with one procedure listed per pocket. • Laminate sentence strips in different colors. • One pocket chart can be used for each area/center in the room. • Yellow sentence strips outline the procedure students follow for the activity or center, including cleaning up the area. • Blue sentence strips indicate activities/assignments that students must complete. • Orange sentence strips are extra-credit activities students may do after completing the required assignment. • Other colored strips can be used to designate both materials needed and student roles. • The pocket chart can be changed to meet the content. • The key is explained to students and is displayed to provide students with a visual reminder. • Students are given opportunities to practice the procedures in order to clarify appropriate noise levels and classroom movement.
Students who get sick during class	• If a student gets sick in class, he/she may go directly to the school nurse. • Other students are asked to make sure the teacher knows if someone leaves the room when sick. • If a student requests a visit to the nurse, the teacher completes a pass to the nurse. The student returns the signed pass to the classroom. The pass is filed in the student's individual file.
Using pencil sharpener	• The first student to arrive in the morning for each group sharpens pencils for the entire group. • Pencils may not be sharpened at any other time of the day.

INSTRUCTIONAL TIME	MY PROCEDURE
Listing assignments/ homework/due dates	• A classroom agenda is used to list the sequence of subjects/events for the day, along with the anticipated time required for each. • The list is created in a sequential manner beneath a clock. • At the end of each subject taught, the assignment is added to the list, and a check is placed next to the completed item, using a different color of marker for each. • Students copy the assignment into individual agendas/homework folders. • The teacher and students discuss the connection to time as appropriate.

Systematically monitoring student learning during instruction	• One method used to monitor student progress is response cards.
	  o One card has *yes* written on it; the other has *no.*
	  o During instruction, the teacher asks students to respond to a question.
	  o Students face forward and place the answer to the question on their forehead. The teacher is able to do a quick visual assessment.
	• The teacher observes while moving from student to student.
	• Anecdotal notes can be kept in a file folder, with an index card for each student taped to the inside of the folder. The teacher moves around the room and interacts with students and makes dated notations on each card. The teacher reviews the cards to make sure each student has had an opportunity to interact with the teacher.
	• Use checklists to record student data.

ENDING CLASS	MY PROCEDURE
Putting things away	• Music is played, or a timer is set, as students work together to clean up the group's community supply holder and floor area around their individual desks. • One person in each group is designated as the checker. When the music stops or the timer beeps, everyone in the group should be finished cleaning up and sitting quietly at his/her desk.
Dismissing class	• Review homework for the day, with students using the agenda or calendar. • Have each student put all books/homework on top of his/her desk. • Students work together to clean up community supply holder and floor area around their individual desks. • To show they're ready, students sit down and put head on desk, with no talking. • Have one group at a time get backpacks and put books and homework into the backpack. Students sit quietly when finished. • Have the student line leader check each group area for completion. The first group finished gets to be first in line behind the line leader.
Collecting papers and assignments	• Each subject has a labeled basket in the room. • As students place their assignments in the appropriate basket, they mark a check on an assignment chart—or one student is in charge of checking in all assignments on a checklist. Each student's name is marked on a checklist to show that the assignment is in the basket.

OTHER	MY PROCEDURE
Lining up for lunch/recess/ special events	• Students work together to clean up community supplies holder and floor area around their individual desks. • To show they're ready, students sit down and put head on desk, with no talking. • Have one group at a time get coats. Students sit down when finished. • Have the student line leader check each group area for completion. The first group finished gets to be first in line behind the line leader.
Walking to lunch/recess	• Students walk quietly in the hall without touching others. • Students may wave at a teacher, but they are not to speak to the teacher.
Putting away coats and backpacks	• Before entering the classroom, students hang backpacks and coats outside the room and quickly move into the classroom. • The teacher stands at the door to greet students as they arrive.
Cleaning out locker/desk	• During a work time or a designated time during the week, a timer is passed from student to student. • When a student receives the timer, he/she sets the timer for five minutes. • The student cleans out his/her desk by putting items on the chair and not the floor. When finished, the student picks up the floor area around his/her desk. • When the timer rings, the student finishes and passes the timer to the next student. The cleaning process continues until all desks are clean.

OTHER	MY PROCEDURE
Preparing for fire drills and/or bomb threats	• Information regarding fire drills and bomb threats is posted in every classroom. • When a fire-drill alarm sounds, students immediately stop their activity and line up at the door. • Students follow the teacher outside, without talking. • At the beginning of each school year, spend time practicing with students.
Going to gym for assemblies/pep rallies	• Over the intercom, grade levels are called to the gym. • Review behavior expectations for the gym. • Students line up following the classroom procedure. • Students walk quietly in the hall and sit in the assigned area in the gym. • The teacher sits among his/her students and monitors behavior during the assembly.
Respecting teacher's desk and storage areas	• Students are taught life skills, such as respect, caring, and responsibility. Teachers use real-life experiences as examples. • Respect for each individual's possessions and body are included in the discussion. • The storage areas for the teacher and students are separate. The teacher's storage is outside the room or behind the teacher's desk. Student storage areas are easily accessed by students. • The teacher prepares a folder (such as this one) for substitutes that outlines classroom procedures, including the materials and storage areas that students are allowed to use.

OTHER	MY PROCEDURE
Appropriately handling/using computers/equipment	• Procedures for using the computers are posted in the computer area. o Work quietly. o Use headphones for sound. o Set the timer for the designated time. o Work with a partner. o Stay in appropriate areas/websites on the computer. • The teacher writes each student's name on a tongue depressor. Use two containers—one labeled "My Turn" and the other "I'm Done." • The teacher chooses the first two partners to work at the computer. • The student chooses a name from the My Turn container as he/she finishes at the computer. When the student is finished, his/her tongue depressor is placed in the container marked I'm Done.

STUDENT ACCOUNTABILITY	MY PROCEDURE
Late work	• Each day before recess, the teacher checks the assignment checklists of the morning and previous afternoon. • The student is given extra time during recess to work on unfinished assignments. A teacher is assigned to the workroom to answer questions and assist with unfinished assignments. • Students completing all assignments for the week receive extra recess time. • Students not completing all assignments will finish assignments during the extra recess time. A teacher will assist students as needed. • At the end of the week, a note is sent home to parents to indicate (1) that all assignments were completed for the week or (2) a list of assignments not completed for the week.

STUDENT ACCOUNTABILITY	MY PROCEDURE
Missing work	• Each day before recess, the teacher checks the assignment checklists of the morning and previous afternoon. • The student is given extra time during recess to work on unfinished assignments. A teacher is assigned to the workroom to answer questions and assist with unfinished assignments. • Students completing all assignments for the week receive extra recess time. • Students not completing all assignments will finish assignments during the extra recess time. • At the end of the week, a note is sent home to the parents to indicate (1) that all assignments were completed for the week or (2) a list of assignments not completed for the week.
Extra credit	• There are limited extra-credit opportunities, but if a student wishes to improve, his/her grade assignments with low scores may be redone. • Students receive 3 extra-credit points for the correct heading on papers.
Redoing work and/or retaking tests	• Interventions are determined for students failing to meet mastery. • Students are placed in skill-based small groups and are taught the concepts with a different instructional approach. • New assignments are completed and scored. In order to learn, students are given more time and instruction.

STUDENT ACCOUNTABILITY	MY PROCEDURE
Incomplete work	• Each day before recess, the teacher reviews the assignment checklists of the morning and the previous afternoon. • The student is given extra time during recess to work on unfinished assignments. A teacher is assigned to the workroom to answer questions and assist with unfinished assignments. • Students completing all assignment for the week receive extra recess time. • Students not completing all assignments will finish assignments during the extra recess time. • At the end of the week, a note is sent home to parents to indicate (1) that all assignments were completed for the week or (2) a list of assignments not completed for the week.
Neatness	• Neatness is strongly encouraged, but assignments are accepted if the teacher can read the assignment. • Students may use computers to help complete assignments.
Papers with no names	• As papers are turned in, students place a check beside their name on an assignment checklist. • Papers with no names are put in a basket labeled "Mr./Ms. No Name." • Use a picture of a unique character above the basket. • A student checker places a check beside the name of the student turning in an assignment. Students without an assignment are quietly reminded that no assignment was turned in for that subject. • The student may look in the Mr./Ms. No Name basket.

STUDENT ACCOUNTABILITY	MY PROCEDURE
Using pens, pencils, colored markers	• Special materials are kept in supply baskets by category. Example: writing materials. • The supply baskets are kept in a specific location in the classroom. • When a supply basket is needed, a designated student from each group will pick one up for his/her group. • When students are finished, the group will clean up the supply basket and return it to the specific location.
Using computer-generated products	• At school students will complete assignments requiring a computer-generated product. • No computer assignments are given as homework. • Extra time will be provided as needed to complete assignments at school.
Internet access on computers	• Students always work with assigned partners. • Peer tutoring may be used to teach computer skills. • One student is taught the skill. He/she teaches the next student. Students repeat the process until all students have been taught. • Each student has the opportunity to teach or peer-tutor another student in the class. • Write each student's name in the class on a tongue depressor. • Use two containers—one labeled My Turn and the other I'm Done. • Each peer tutor chooses a name from the My Turn container and teaches that student. When the student is finished, the tongue depressor is placed in the container marked I'm Done.

<table>
<tr><th>STUDENT ACCOUNTABILITY</th><th>MY PROCEDURE</th></tr>
<tr><td>Setting and assigning due dates</td><td><ul><li>Create a monthly calendar in the classroom on a large white board.</li><li>On the white board write assignments in green, when final projects are due in blue, and components of the project that are due on different days in red.</li><li>Post a key beside the calendar.</li><li>Mark the date on the calendar as assignments are due.</li><li>At the end of each day, a student leader transfers the assignments from the agenda to the calendar.</li><li>To plan backward for a project with several components, give each student a paper calendar stapled to a file folder or large manila envelope.</li><li>The entire class plans together for long-term projects. Students write the assignment component on the calendar date as decided by the class. Use the file folder/envelope to store the components of the project as completed.</li></ul></td></tr>
<tr><td>Writing on back of paper</td><td><ul><li>Students may write on the back of the paper.</li></ul></td></tr>
<tr><td>Makeup work and amount of time for makeup work</td><td><ul><li>Assignments for the week are to be completed by the end of the day on Friday. Exceptions are made for absences if the student or parent request more time.</li><li>A note is sent home each week to inform the parent of completed and/or incomplete assignments.</li></ul></td></tr>
<tr><td>Letting students know assignments missed during absence</td><td><ul><li>Folders with all assignments are created for students when absent from school.</li><li>Assignments are generally due the next day or later if more than one day is missed. Students and/or parents may request more time.</li></ul></td></tr>
</table>

STUDENT ACCOUNTABILITY	MY PROCEDURE
Letting students know assignments missed during absence *(continued)*	• It is the student's responsibility to request, complete, and turn in assignments. If that isn't done by the end of the week, a note will be sent home on Friday, noting the assignment(s) to be completed. • Parents and students are informed at the beginning of the school year, during parent/teacher conferences, and throughout the year as needed.
Percentage of grade for major tests, homework, etc.	• Homework is limited. If homework is sent home, it is checked for completion. • Check with other teachers at the grade level to create grading consistency for all students at the grade level. • Locate a copy of the school grading policy.
Explaining your grading policy	• Grading policy is explained to parents and students at the beginning of the school year and throughout the year as needed.
Letting new students know your procedures	• Create a procedure notebook for each student in the classroom. • Include a copy of each classroom procedure. • Give a new student a copy. • Explain the classroom procedures to the new student. • As necessary, refer to the appropriate procedure and have the student locate the procedure in the notebook. • Have the student write his/her understanding of the procedure. • Assign a classroom friend to assist the student with classroom procedures. • Have other students role-play or model the procedures for the new student.

STUDENT ACCOUNTABILITY	MY PROCEDURE
Having contact with all students at least once during week	• Greet each student as he/she enters the room. • Use Popsicle sticks, each with a different student name, to call on students during class. • Create a seating chart and make a new copy for each week. Record brief notes, subject, and date as you interact with each student. On Thursday, target students without evidence of interaction.
Exchanging papers	• There are limited opportunities for students to exchange papers. • When papers are exchanged, students must put pencils away and get a colored pencil, crayon, or pen. • The teacher might Velcro a colored pen to the side of each student's desk. • Students put their initials in the top left corner of the paper. • Students mark correct answers with a check. Count the number correct and put +10 at the top of the paper underneath the initials.
Using Internet for posting assignments and sending them in	• Students will complete assignments requiring a computer-generated product at school. • No computer assignments will be given as homework. • Extra time will be provided as needed to complete assignments. • Students may e-mail an assignment to the teacher as the teacher assigns.

HOW WILL YOU ...	MY PLAN
Determine grades on report cards (components and weights of those components)?	• Grades are not weighted.
Grade daily assignments?	• Assignments are graded and returned to students on a daily basis.
Record grades so that assignments and dates are included?	• Grades are recorded in the gradebook. List the assignment and date at the top of the gradebook.
Have students keep records of their own grades?	• Students keep a binder with a variety of materials. Divide the binder into tabs. • One tab has a blank grade sheet for each subject area taught. • Each student records grades on the appropriate gradesheet as papers are returned. • At the end of the grading period, the students receive rewards for recording all grades correctly. Examples: extra points, a special activity, lunch with the teacher, note to parents praising responsible behavior. • Students may use the gradesheets to set and monitor personal learning goals. • Students may also create progress reports on teacher-created blank progress reports to take home for parents to sign.
Make sure your assignments and grading reflect progress against standards?	• The grade-level teachers grid student test data to determine the focus of instruction. • Using the information from the data grids, grade-level teams align time and content to determine the standards to be taught each quarter. • Use 10-question-test benchmarks to measure student progress during each quarter. • Teachers create interventions to support student mastery of standards.

HOW WILL YOU …	MY PLAN
Notify parents when students are not passing or having other academic problems?	• Send a note home each week to inform parents of completed or missing assignments. • First, share a positive, then the concern when contacting parents with an academic concern. • Share with parents the interventions tried or planned.
Contact parents if problem arises regarding student behavior?	• Meet or phone every parent at the beginning of the school year to build rapport. Make sure the first call made to parents is positive. • Communicate a positive along with the concern. • The teacher keeps a record of discipline interventions made at school to teach the student choice and consequence, then shares with the parents. • Ask the parents to provide insight and suggestions for changing the inappropriate behavior. • Contact parents the day of the problem. • If possible, have the student phone a parent and explain the problem. Talk to the parent after the student finishes.
Contact parents with positive feedback about their child?	• Contact parents of each student at the beginning of the school year to introduce yourself. Have parents share information about the student. • Send home a monthly newsletter to share classroom news and announcements. • When talking to a parent about a concern, start and end with a positive. • Send a personal note home for each student at least once a month. Keep a record of these notes.

HOW WILL YOU ...	MY PLAN
Keep records and documentation of student behavior?	• Use a checklist with a numbered list of possible student behaviors. • Keep the checklist on a clipboard in an easily accessible location. • Record the number of the behavior by the student's name on the checklist. List the date at the top of the list. • Use the record to send positive notes home for students for good or improving behavior.
Document adherence to IEP (individualized education plan)?	• Meet with the special education teacher on a monthly basis to discuss student progress and concerns. • Create a checklist of goals/modifications for the student. The teacher monitors and records his/her adherence to the IEP, as well as notes student successes. • Keep a copy in a folder in the back of planbook. Refer to planbook when planning for the week in order to differentiate instruction to meet all student-learning needs.
Return graded papers in timely manner?	• Some assignments are checked for completion. • Attempt to return graded items daily or determine a day that papers will be returned in a group. • Be consistent and provide feedback that supports student learning.

HOW WILL YOU …	MY PLAN
Monitor students who have serious health issues (peanut allergies, diabetes, epilepsy, etc.)?	• Work with the parent to create an emergency plan for each student with a serious health concern (or concerns). • Discuss with students in the classroom as appropriate. • Example: Student is allergic to bee stings. o A parent attends all out-of-school field trips. o The student goes to the art room during recess as needed. o If a bee enters the classroom, the student leaves the room immediately and goes to the nurse to wait until a student from the class comes and gets him/her. o The teacher learns how to use an epi-pen to stop allergic reactions—and keeps one in the classroom.

CHAPTER FOUR

DISCIPLINE STRATEGIES: GRADES 6–8

GENERAL COMMENTS ABOUT MIDDLE SCHOOL

In middle school the basic issues are that students are making the transition from being cared for to taking care of themselves. Part of taking care of yourself is being organized. So a huge chunk of time is spent in middle school teaching students how to be organized. Consistency is a big issue in organization, and so it's important, particularly in middle school, that there be a team approach to the grade level—and that a consistent approach be used for organization, behavior, and expectations.

A second issue in middle school is the maturity of the students. Hormones are "raging," and identity is shifting. So your friend on Monday will not necessarily by your friend on Tuesday—but could very possibly be your friend on Wednesday. Sexual information is at a premium, and what it means to be an adolescent is constantly changing. If the campus and classroom can be generally predictable and consistent, it makes a huge difference for students.

A few students already are parents themselves—yes, in middle school. Your approach to the student is of the utmost importance, and it's helpful to be predominantly in the adult voice (see Appendix, page 138). In short, your classroom *system* will make or break you in middle school.

What management tools do you give students?

If you simply require that 20% of the grade be based on the processes that students use, and 80% be based on content understanding, you will see a significant jump in achievement.

	STRATEGIES
1.	Planning backward
2.	Planning their grade
3.	Syllabi, calendars, datelines, planners
4.	3×5 cards
5.	System involving manila folders and envelopes
6.	Step sheets
7.	Color coding
8.	Graphic organizers

What do you do when a student will not finish or hand in work?

STEPS	ACTION
1.	*Teach the whole class* time management and planning backward. For example, if an assignment is due on Friday, what day must students start working? In addition, have students plan what grades they intend to receive in each class.
2.	Talk to the student one on one if possible and communicate through "sticky notes."
3.	Assess the reasons for the work not being done.
4.	Ask for a plan from the student about when the work can be completed. Identify the smaller, in-between steps to get it done.
5.	Identify the consequences of work not being completed.

ASK YOURSELF ...

1. Can the student read?
2. Is the student the primary support system for several other individuals at home?
3. Does the student have a child of her own?
4. Is the student moving from place to place?
5. Was a step sheet provided for the student to finish the work?
6. How is the assignment relevant to the student's motivation?
7. Is the student given opportunities to work with other students?

What do you do when students are mean to each other or you?

STEPS	ACTION
1.	Explain that manners actually help people live together without embarrassing each other or themselves. Research demonstrates that achievement is higher when students and teachers are courteous with each other.
2.	Identify the phrases you expect to hear in your classroom. Translate from the casual register to the formal. Example: "He is an ass." The translation might be: "I find him to be a difficult person."
3.	Model the kinds of courtesies you wish to hear. Examples: "Please be seated" and "I'm sorry, I couldn't hear what you said; please repeat it for me."
4.	Decide when the rude and impolite behavior interrupts the learning and when it can be ignored. (Not every incident in the classroom must be addressed; most teachers find they need to "pick their battles.")

ASK YOURSELF …

1. Is this "the norm" in your classroom?
2. Is this a problem for only a few students?
3. Is there a rivalry between a couple of students or groups of students? Are gangs a problem in your school?
4. Have you explained the importance of manners?
5. Does the student know and use manners outside of school?
6. Are *you* rude or impolite to students?
7. If you are sarcastic, are students allowed to be sarcastic back to you?
8. Is the student on medication, being abused, without role models, socially isolated?

How do you handle a bully?

Bullying is both a system issue and an individual issue. In organizational research we find the concept of "isomorphism," which means that what happens at one level of the organization tends to happen at all levels. So if you have student bullies, you likely have teacher bullies and administrator bullies. In most school systems, student bullying is a zero-tolerance activity.

STEPS	ACTION
1.	Identify the action or behavior that was unacceptable.
2.	Ask this question: "When you did that, what did you want or need?"
3.	Identify alternative behavior(s).
4.	Recommend/require that the bully get involved in some type of supervised community service.
5.	Refer the case to the administration.

How do you handle the instigator—the student who creates many of the problems?

It's important to understand how an instigator works. First of all, instigators love omissions, the part of the story that is not told. And the instigator almost always uses sexual innuendo and insult. This can be verbal or nonverbal. Nonverbal messages often are used because they allow the instigator to be "innocent." Instigators also use a divide-and-conquer strategy; in other words, I'll tell you one thing and tell the other person something else.

If you wish to identify who your campus instigators are, a simple tool is available. Give every teacher and staff person a disposable camera. When there's a fight, the staff members take pictures.

Students scatter almost immediately. But usually the instigators are watching the fight, and they're in most of the pictures of the fight.

To end the behavior, the following steps often help.

STEPS	ACTION
1.	First, talk individually to the students. This is the key question: *"Were you there when they said/did that?"* Almost always they weren't present; it was reported back to them.
2.	Ask who told them. Typically they won't tell you—particularly if it's a school bully. So you can say: *"Did you have a vision?"* At that point they often will tell you the person's name.
3.	Repeat Steps 1 and 2 with the next person. You tend to get the same name(s). This is your instigator.
4.	Put the instigator between the two individuals and ask each of them to tell the other what the instigator told them. Very quickly they hear the omission.
5.	If you want to end the behavior of the instigator, the instigator must receive the same consequences as the individuals who got into trouble as a result of the instigation.

What do you do when a student cheats?

STEPS	ACTION
1.	Document the activity.
2.	Give a zero.
3.	Sometimes teachers will give a test or alternative activity to find out what learning has occurred.
4.	Determine the intervention based on the reason(s) for cheating.

ASK YOURSELF …

What is the "payoff" for cheating?

- A passing grade
- Reduced anxiety about tests
- Less pressure from parents

How do you handle the student who is inappropriately sexual (jokes, stories, gestures, etc.)?

STEPS	ACTION
1.	*Teach the whole class* (at least five minutes) about sexual-harassment laws, guidelines, and the seriousness of the law, particularly as it relates to required consequences at school and work.
2.	Strictly forbid sexual harassment in your classroom.
3.	Document the specific behaviors/comments in writing.
4.	Refer the student to the administration.
5.	If a student sexually harasses others repeatedly, it may be an indicator of sexual abuse. In this case the student also needs to be referred to a counselor, nurse, administrator, etc.

PROCEDURES CHECKLIST: GRADES 6–8

The following checklist for Grades 6–8 has been adapted from Guidelines for the First Days of School from the Research Development Center for Teacher Education, Research on Classrooms, University of Texas, Austin.

Karen Miller, Grapevine, Texas, prepared this sample checklist.

STARTING CLASS	MY PROCEDURE
Taking attendance	• Students are assigned seats. Seats are numbered, and students are assigned numbers. • The teacher has a seating chart for each period. The seating chart consists of small Post-its with the student's name and a small photograph if necessary, and these are attached to a plan of the desks in the classroom. (Photographs are obtained from the yearbook and the attendance list from the computer.) • The teacher can take attendance using the chart while the students are working on their warm-ups. Data are entered into the computer. • For the first week of school students call out their names as teacher checks the chart to help with pronunciation and association. • Post-it notes are moved around when new seats are assigned.
Marking absences	• Attendance is marked on a class list for teacher reference, after which the data are transferred to the computer or an attendance slip that is posted on the door to be picked up by the office aide.
Tardy students	• A tardy sheet is placed on a clipboard by the door. There's a class list for each period, which is replaced each grading period. • If students enter the class late, they stop and sign the tardy board: date, name, and reason. If there's a note, they attach it to the board as well.

STARTING CLASS	MY PROCEDURE
Tardy students *(continued)*	• When the teacher has time, he/she checks the tardy list and has a private discussion with the student. • The consequences of the school tardy policy are followed. • Each grading period the student is allowed one free tardy with a warning; a second tardy would result in a teacher detention; and a third is an office detention, with parent notification. Before this level is reached, however, an intervention is normally in place to solve the problem. • Students with no tardies enter their names into a container, and a drawing for a reward is made each week.
Giving makeup work for absentees	• Absentee folders are available. Each folder contains the following: "Missed Assignment" sheet, "We Missed You" note, and makeup work policy—how many days students have to get the assignment in to get a full grade, calendar to plan how to accomplish this, etc. • These folders, a hanging file holder for worksheets, a school planner, and a monthly calendar are placed in an assigned area of the room. • Class assignments are recorded daily in the planner by an appointed student, and any necessary worksheets are placed in the hanging folder according to date and period. • As students return to school they pick up a folder and record the missing work. The completed work is returned in the folder, so the folder is reused.
Enrolling new students	• Each period has an assigned, trained class greeter who is responsible for assisting any new student in the classroom. • A folder with classroom procedures, supplies, a plan to show where everything is in the classroom, an "All About Me" form, and a welcome card are given to a new student.

STARTING CLASS	MY PROCEDURE
Enrolling new students *(continued)*	• During the period the teacher meets with the new student. • New-student information is recorded in the computer, and the student is added to the class list and gradebook.
Un-enrolling students	• Follow the school checklist promptly. Final grades are entered, textbooks are returned to the book room, library clearance is checked, and lockers are cleaned out. • A care packet is given to each student who leaves the school.
Students who have to leave school early	• The office sends a notification that the student needs to leave. • The student checks that he/she has everything needed to complete the assignments he/she will miss. • The student signs the "Bye for Now" sheet at the door, including time and date, so the teacher can keep a record of student movement.
Warm-up activity (that students begin as soon as they walk into classroom)	• Students pick up their class folders and necessary supplies as they enter the classroom. Students record in their planners the objectives and activities for the day from the board. • This list becomes a checklist for the period. Students check off completed assignments. • Student then work on the assigned warm-up, which will vary according to the lesson for the day. Examples: journal entry, a challenge, reviewing a concept. • The warm-up is checked, shared, or discussed five minutes after the bell rings. A timer is set.

INSTRUCTIONAL TIME	MY PROCEDURE
Student movement within classroom	• How students are expected to walk around the classroom is modeled and practiced. • Students are taught to use the least distracting route to the pencil sharpener, to hand in papers, to the supply closet, to the pillow area, and to the teacher desk. • Students also practice 30-second breakouts to rearranged desks to facilitate different grouping arrangements. • Music is used as a transition device. There's a cleanup song, a move-to-your-groups song, or activity song. By the end of the song, the students need to be in the assigned area ready to work.
Use of cell phones and headphones	• Cell phones and headphones are not allowed in classrooms. • First offense: The student receives a warning and returns the phone or headphones to his/her locker. • Second offense: The phone or headphones are removed and taken to the office where a parent would have to retrieve them. • If listening to music has been earned as a reward, the student has permission to bring the headphones to the teacher's room for that period only.
Student movement in and out of classroom	• Entering and exiting the classroom is practiced frequently at the start of the school year and is revisited as needed. • The movement is orderly and respectful of others. Students line up outside the classroom during passing period until the teacher opens the door. Incoming students enter in single file as the teacher stands at the door greeting students. • Students follow warm-up procedures that have been modeled and practiced. Voices are low until the bell rings, then the class is silent in order to hear the directions for the day. • The teacher, not the bell, dismisses the class, so students are to remain in their seats and engaged in learning until the teacher dismisses them—either row by row or team by team.

INSTRUCTIONAL TIME	MY PROCEDURE
Going to restroom	• Students need a pass to be in the hallway during class periods. • Teachers sign a student planner and write down the time the student leaves the room. If the student has no planner and needs to go to the restroom, the teacher could write a pass. The teacher monitors how many times a student is leaving the room by having a signout/signin sheet at the door. • If it's a daily occurrence, the teacher and student have a conference and discuss other alternatives.
Getting students' attention	• "High five" hand signal—silent in five seconds • Lights on/off • Chimes/instruments • Claps
Students talking during class	• Time to talk in a structured way is built into the lesson. Some of the methods are "Talking Chips," round robin (timed sharing around a group), "Pair Share," peer coaching, 30-second share. • Voice levels are practiced, and hand movements and analogies are used to indicate noise level permitted. Example: Six-inch voices, with hand movement to match. • Background music sets the loudness of the voices allowed; no voice is to be heard over the music.
What students do when their work is completed	• A list of "Things to Do" when students have completed their work is posted in the classroom. There's a variety of activities—many of them rewarding to encourage students to stay on task and complete their classwork. • A "lounging" area to work in also is available in the classroom.

INSTRUCTIONAL TIME	MY PROCEDURE
Working together as group(s)	• If working in pairs or groups is used as a teaching tool, then students are assigned to groups by the teacher. Roles are determined, and cards are handed out to explain each student's role and accountability in the group. • The social aspects of working successfully with a group are taught and reinforced. • The group has clear objectives and outcomes. • Informal groups or pairs are a useful tool to promote student interaction. • Group work needs to be carefully monitored by the teacher. The task needs to be well-defined, and a time limit for task completion is assigned to prevent off-task behavior.
Handing in papers/homework	• Each classroom has a clearly labeled basket where students place their work. • A group checklist may be used to monitor any missing assignments immediately.
Appropriate headings for papers	• The heading format is posted in the room for reference. • The heading is consistent throughout the school. • Five points of the grade are allocated to the heading. • With a star students mark the center spot on their paper where the heading is to go. "You Are a Star" is one way for students to remember this.
Bringing/distributing/ using textbooks	• After textbooks have been distributed to students during a designated class period, they bring their books to the classroom. The books' numbers are recorded on a class book list by the student, then checked by the teacher. • The contents of the books are covered in class, and the students do a scavenger hunt to familiarize themselves with the format of the book, as well as the sections. • If the teacher has a class set, the textbooks are taken home.

INSTRUCTIONAL TIME	MY PROCEDURE
Bringing/distributing/ using textbooks *(continued)*	• A poster is placed next to each classroom door listing supplies/books that are needed for that class. • A color is associated with different books and activities. • Extra books are kept in the classroom so that students may check them out.
Leaving room for special class	• Students sign a "Signout Sheet" at the door: date, time, reason.
Students who don't have paper and/or pencils	• A team box with supplies for each team is available. The material monitor is responsible for checking his/her team box before class starts and before class is dismissed. • Sharpened, marked (colored tape, silk flowers) pencils and pens are placed near the pencil sharpener for use during class. These are to be returned after class. Paper is available in a paper tray in a designated area. Students donate paper to keep the supply going. • Students are responsible to have the supplies they need before class starts, so that learning time isn't lost. • An after-school homework club every afternoon is open for students who need extra help or supplies for project work.
Signal(s) for getting student attention	• "High five" hand signal • Lights • Chimes • Clapping
Touching other students in classroom	• "Keep your hands, feet, and objects to yourself" shows respect for others and is enforced. • Students who cannot follow the above rule are moved away from the person they are bothering. Routes in the room are defined and practiced until an improvement is noted. • A private student/teacher discussion establishes other ways to show feelings or resolve conflict. Replacement behaviors are decided upon and practiced.

INSTRUCTIONAL TIME	MY PROCEDURE
Eating food in classroom	• Food is not allowed in the classroom. Water is allowed. • If a teacher supplies snacks as a reward, they have to be eaten during that teacher's class period. • The late-lunch grade level has an assigned snack period where the students could bring a healthy snack to class. A list of suggested snack items is discussed, distributed, and posted in all classrooms.
Laboratory procedures (materials and supplies, safety routines, cleaning up)	• The district guidelines are followed. • Demonstrations take place, and the students have to pass the safety test before they can participate in the labs.
Students who get sick during class	• The teacher fills in a "Nurse Pass" that provides the date, time, reason, and teacher's name. The student then reports to the nurse's office. • If the student returns, the pass returns with the student informing the teacher of the result of the visit. • If the student is sent home, the teacher is called and informed. • If a student is too ill to get to the nurse's office, the nurse is called and the student is escorted to the office.
Using pencil sharpener	• Pencils are sharpened before class starts. • If a pencil breaks during class and the teacher is talking, the student exchanges his/her pencil for a sharpened pencil from the "Pencil/Pen Can." When the instruction part of the lesson is complete, the student may then sharpen his/her pencil. • The teacher models why this is necessary by sharpening a pencil while giving directions. The students can't hear! The point is obvious. • Rule: Only one person at the pencil sharpener at any given time.

INSTRUCTIONAL TIME	MY PROCEDURE
Listing assignments/ homework/due dates	• A large, bulletin-size calendar is used to display assignment-due days, upcoming events. • This calendar also is used to model back planning of long-term assignments. • Homework lists are kept on a weekly board so students can keep a checklist for themselves.
Systematically monitoring student learning during instruction	• The teacher moves around the room during the period monitoring student work by tallying on-task behavior, spot-checking work, and giving immediate feedback. • Students have self-corrective stations set up in the classroom where they go to check their work periodically during the class period: Sticker if all right, make corrections if not writing down where the mistake was found. • The timer is set; when it goes off students turn to a partner and check their answers, as well as share their thoughts or observations.

ENDING CLASS	MY PROCEDURE
Putting things away	• A cleanup song is played and students return their books/folders/supplies, areas are straightened up, and students need to be back in their seats with their agendas displayed for closure.
Dismissing class	• The agenda is used to review the learning that has taken place during the period. Students check completed assignments and circle those to be completed for homework. They make a list of supplies needed in order to complete the task. If there's no planner, this is done on an index card. An exit pass is sometimes required. • The teacher does a quick walk-through and dismisses students as they are finished. • The teacher, not the bell, dismisses the students. The process is practiced daily until it is mastered.

ENDING CLASS	MY PROCEDURE
Collecting papers and assignments	• Each period has a "Hand In" basket. A check of the list is completed at the end of the period to see who has missing work. • Work handed in on time receives a rubber stamp and is clipped together. Each day has a different stamp. • Group checklists can be used. • For a quick collection of classwork, students pass the papers to the person at the back of the row or an assigned group number. That student then checks papers for names and hands all the papers into the designated area.

OTHER	MY PROCEDURE
Lining up for lunch/recess/special events	• The students line up and move on the right side of the hallways. • They are expected to walk in order to minimize disruption of other classes.
Walking to lunch/recess	• All teachers walk the students to and from lunch for the first two weeks of school to ensure that the students know what the expectations are for this process. The same hallway rules apply. • The teachers on duty monitor after this.
Putting away coats and backpacks	• Students are required to put backpacks and coats into lockers in the morning; they aren't removed until the end of the school day. • Students carry their supplies and books to class.
Cleaning out locker	• Periodic locker "cleaning out" days are scheduled by each grade level during an advisory time. • A lost-property box is placed in the hallway for items found. • An extra-supplies box also is available for extra school supplies.

OTHER	MY PROCEDURE
Preparing for fire drills and/or bomb threats	• Each teacher has a procedures flipbook with all the steps needed for each kind of disaster. The book is kept on a clipboard with an updated class list for each period, missing-student form, and a pen that hangs by the classroom door. • This clipboard goes with the teacher. • These drills are practiced as an entire school. • Each teacher instructs his/her advisory class on the process and procedures.
Going to gym for assemblies/pep rallies	• Grade levels are called over the intercom in staggered order. • Teachers escort their classes to the gym and are responsible for their students during the assembly or rally. • Students do not bring backpacks to the gym.
Respecting teacher's desk and storage areas	• The class has a "family meeting" at the beginning of the year when various class topics are discussed—such as respect and what that looks like and sounds like in the classroom. • The teacher's desk is discussed. The parameters are clearly explained. When the teacher is absent, the drawers should be locked. • A substitute folder and supply box is left on the desk. • Respecting other students' property also is discussed. • One storage closet or area is filled with student supplies and is available to all students. • A second closet or area contains teacher supplies and is not to be used without permission. It is kept locked. • Displaying family photographs and various students' gifts helps build a relationship with the students.

OTHER	**MY PROCEDURE**
Appropriately handling/using computers/equipment	• Rules and procedures are posted at the computers. • Students sign a log when they're using the computer. • How to use a computer is modeled and reinforced. • Incorrect usage results in immediate removal of a student. Any offending students will get another chance the next day after completing a sheet to show that they understand what they did wrong and how they'll correct the behavior. • If a student is caught on an inappropriate website, he/she loses all computer rights at school. • Computers are available to use for school assignments after school with teacher supervision.

STUDENT ACCOUNTABILITY	**MY PROCEDURE**
Late work	• Students lose 10% a day for late work. • After three days, the teacher arranges a time for the student to stay before or after school to complete the assignment.
Missing work	• The teacher keeps a running list of missing work. The student is informed and invited to a before- or after-school homework club to complete assignments. Parents are contacted as the teacher deems necessary. • Zeros are not tolerated. • Extra worksheets are kept in a hanging folder so students can get extra copies of missing or lost assignments.

STUDENT ACCOUNTABILITY	MY PROCEDURE
Missing work *(continued)*	• Students are shown their grades weekly. With guidance from the teacher they calculate their present grade and what they need to pass the class or achieve a higher grade. This planning helps the student to make the transition from the abstraction of grades to the concrete (their assignment). It helps students to see that they have control over their grades and ultimately over their success or failure in school.
Extra credit	• Extra-credit assignments are available so that students can improve their grades. • The teacher supplies the choices for the extra-credit assignments, as well as a grading rubric, the number of points available, and the due date. • The extra credit is the student's responsibility to hand in.
Redoing work and/or retaking tests	• Learning is the objective, and the correction of mistakes and redoing tasks are vital parts of the learning process—so students have every opportunity to redo work or tests. • They receive half credit for corrected or completed work.
Incomplete work	• Students are aware of the grading procedure or evaluation tool that will be used to grade their work. • Handing in an incomplete assignment will cost them grade-wise, but it will avoid a zero. • A private conference with a student about the incomplete assignment takes place when the assignment is returned, and a plan to complete the next assignment will be discussed. • If the student expresses a desire to better his/her grade by redoing the assignment, it is accepted.

STUDENT ACCOUNTABILITY	MY PROCEDURE
Neatness	• All work is expected to be neat. • Grades are not docked because of lack of neatness. However, a student will be warned. The next assignment might have to be redone.
Papers with no names	• Papers are placed in an area that is labeled by periods so students can search for their work if it is missing. • This area is cleaned out at the beginning of each new grading period. • Students lose grades for not having a heading (5 points). • A plan is decided on to prevent this from happening repeatedly.
Using pens, pencils, colored markers	• Pens and pencils are used for all schoolwork. Markers are for decorating or highlighting a point. Students hand in all markers at the beginning of the school year, and the teacher puts boxes out as needed.
Using computer-generated products	• The use of computer-generated products is acceptable where indicated by the teacher. • Students receive training on different computer programs available at the school. • Technology is incorporated into lessons and assignments. • Computer labs are booked in advance so all students have equal opportunity to complete assignments.
Internet access on computers	• Students are trained and rules are taught. • Security locks prevent students from accessing certain sites. • Students may not use computers unless a teacher is present.
Setting and assigning due dates	• The teaching team meets and ensures that the calendar is well-coordinated as far as due dates for projects and tests are concerned. • School events are taken into consideration.

STUDENT ACCOUNTABILITY	MY PROCEDURE
Writing on back of paper	• Students have permission to do this.
Makeup work and amount of time for makeup work	• Students are allowed the number of days they were absent plus one day to hand in missed assignments. • Student gets makeup work from each teacher.
Letting students know assignments missed during absence	• If a parent contacts the school and wants work to be sent home, then each teacher records the missed assignments (and includes any necessary worksheets) and sends the information to the Attendance Office. • Absentee folders are created. Each folder contains the following: Missed Assignment sheet, We Missed You note, and makeup work policy—how many days students have to get the assignment in to get a full grade, calendar to plan how to accomplish this, etc.. • These folders, a hanging file holder, a school planner, and a monthly calendar are placed in an assigned area of the classroom. • Class assignments are recorded daily in the planner by an appointed student, and any necessary worksheets are placed in the hanging folder according to date and period. • As students return to school they pick up a folder and record the missing work. The completed work is returned in the folder, so the folder is reused.
Percentage of grade for major tests, homework, etc.	• Check with the department chair for your subject and your grade level and the department's weighting system. • The weighting system should be consistent. • Homework should have a maximum weight of 10% of the total grade. • For example: Language Arts— 30% tests and portfolio evaluations 30% daily work and quizzes 30% writing and grammar 10% homework

STUDENT ACCOUNTABILITY	MY PROCEDURE
Explaining your grading policy	• This information was covered in the first days of the new school year on the course description and policy handouts. • Posters explaining the system are also displayed above the area where work is turned in. • The grading policy and procedure are revisited each grading period and with any major assignment.
Letting new students know your procedures	• Each period has an assigned, trained class greeter who is responsible for assisting any new student in the classroom. • A folder with classroom procedures, supplies, a plan to show where everything is in the classroom, an All About Me form, and a welcome card are given to a new student. • During the period I will meet privately with the student.
Having contact with all students at least once during week	• Choose five students per class that you are going to notice—by writing to or talking to each day of the week. • Greet students at the door daily. • Student/teacher conferences about progress and problems each grading period • Meet with students about their accountability test scores. Recognize strengths and discuss weaknesses and ways to improve in those areas. Students will revisit these goals and interventions after each grading period or benchmark test. • Recognize birthdays and special accomplishments, including attendance.
Exchanging papers	• Students do not exchange papers for grading purposes. • Papers are exchanged during the editing process or for peer evaluations. • Students have a detailed rubric and evaluation sheet to ensure that the feedback was constructive and helpful.

STUDENT ACCOUNTABILITY	MY PROCEDURE
Using Internet for posting assignments and sending them in	• Students are able to complete assignments and presentations online. The finished product is sent to a school e-mail address. • The school webpage had classes listed, with weekly assignments and any upcoming projects posted.

HOW WILL YOU ...	MY PLAN
Determine grades on report cards (components and weights of those components)?	• Check with your department chair and also discuss the weighting of grades with your grade-level team. • These should be consistent and explained to the students.
Grade daily assignments?	• These assignments are graded in class at the beginning or near the end of the class. • Corrections are made immediately. • A participation or completion grade can be recorded.
Record grades so that assignments and dates are included?	• A class list run on a blank grid can be used to record grades and dates before entering them into the gradebook or computer. • The sheets are run on a different color for each grading period; this helps the teacher keep up with missing assignments.
Have students keep records of their own grades?	• Students are given a tool for recording their own grades. • The teacher checks in with students and helps them make the connections. This is done weekly with students who are at risk of failing.
Make sure your assignments and grading reflect progress against standards?	• Teachers use data grids, grade-distribution sheets, and time and content grids to evaluate progress or areas of weakness in their program, as well as the needs of their students.

HOW WILL YOU …	MY PLAN
Make sure your assignments and grading reflect progress against standards? *(continued)*	• Ten-question benchmark tests are used to analyze progress and target weak areas both for individual students and the entire class. • This information assists a teacher in planning his/her lessons. Weak classwide standards need to be retaught as a class; individual student weaknesses need to be addressed in tutorial groups.
Notify parents when students are not passing or having other academic problems?	• Parents are informed when their son/daughter is being successful, as well as having difficulties. • Calling home, e-mailing, or home visits are all effective ways of contacting parents. • When informing parents about their child's academic problems, have a plan to address the issue that entails teacher intervention, such as homework club and tutorials.
Contact parents if problem arises regarding student behavior?	• A parent is contacted on major discipline issues that result in referrals. • Minor problems are taken care of at school. • Contact with the parent(s) is made to gain insight into a student's behavior and to seek a solution to correct the behavior. • Each teacher keeps a phone journal, as well as hard copies of e-mails sent home. • Each teacher also keeps a running log of students' discipline problems and the consequences and interventions that were made to correct the problems.
Contact parents with positive feedback about their child?	• A positive note or call home is made during the first weeks of school to every parent by one of the teachers on the grade-level team; this is continued throughout the year. • A biweekly grade-level newspaper can be sent home to keep parents informed. • Information, photographs, and grade-level celebrations can be posted on the school webpage.

HOW WILL YOU …	MY PLAN
Keep records and documentation of student behavior?	• After a behavior problem, a discipline sheet is created for that student. • All contacts home, as well as discipline actions, are recorded. This sheet is kept in a binder—discipline log. • All interventions also are recorded. • All notes sent or received are kept in a folder.
Document adherence to IEP (individualized education plan)?	• The Special Education Department supplies each classroom teacher with a binder containing the IEPs of all the special-needs students she/he teaches. • Modifications are noted. Examples showing how these modifications are being met in the classroom are kept. • IEPs are updated every three weeks. The inclusion teacher meets with the classroom teacher to discuss any concerns. • Grades and progress are monitored.
Return graded papers in timely manner?	• All work is corrected, but not all classwork is graded by the teacher. • Student work is returned on a stated day so parents can be looking for graded work. Turnaround should be as quick as possible. • Corrections can be made and handed in during the week the papers were returned. • Tests are returned to students as quickly as possible.
Monitor students who have serious health issues (peanut allergies, diabetes, epilepsy, etc.)?	• The school nurse supplies the teachers with a list of student health issues. • These issues are confidential but should be readily available for a teacher to refer to when needed. • Keep the list in your lesson plan book on a brightly colored sheet of paper so that it's easily found.

CHAPTER FIVE

DISCIPLINE STRATEGIES: GRADES 9–12

GENERAL COMMENTS ABOUT HIGH SCHOOL

The typical approach at high school is to (1) warn, (2) discuss, (3) give detention, (4) make referral, and (5) notify parents/guardians. Among many high school teachers, mutual respect and humor are used to maintain classroom systems that work.

What do you do when students are impolite or even rude to each other and/or you?

ASK YOURSELF …

1. Is this "the norm" in your classroom?
2. Is this a problem for only a few students?
3. Is there a rivalry between a couple of students or groups of students? Are gangs a problem at your school?
4. Have you explained the importance of manners?
5. Does the student know and use manners outside of school?
6. Are *you* rude or impolite to students?
7. If you are sarcastic, are students allowed to be sarcastic back to you?

STEPS	ACTION
1.	Explain that manners actually help people live together without embarrassing each other or themselves. The research is that achievement is higher when students and teachers are courteous with each other.
2.	Identify the phrases you expect to hear in your classroom. Translate from the casual register to the formal. Example: "He is an ass." The translation might be: "I find him to be a difficult person."
3.	Model the kinds of courtesies you wish to hear. Examples: "Please be seated" and "I'm sorry, I couldn't hear what you said; please repeat it for me."
4.	Decide when the rude and impolite behavior interrupts the learning and when it can be ignored. (Not every incident in the classroom must be addressed; most teachers find they need to "pick their battles.")
5.	Use humor. Example: "He is a *snot* jerk." You say, *"What is a snot jerk? Let's write a dictionary entry for this word. Please give it four different definitions and hand it in to me at the end of class."*
6.	For some students, there must be an outright ban. Say: *"If you persist, then you have chosen."*

What management tools do you give students?

If you simply require that 20% of the grade be based on the processes that students use, and 80% be based on content understanding, you will see a significant jump in achievement.

	STRATEGIES
1.	Planning backward
2.	Planning their grades
3.	Syllabi, calendars, datelines, planners
4.	3×5 cards
5.	System involving manila folders and envelopes
6.	Step sheets
7.	Color coding
8.	Graphic organizers

What do you do when a student will not finish or hand in work?

ASK YOURSELF …

1. Does the student work full time?
2. Can the student read?
3. Is the student the primary support system for several other individuals at home?
4. Does the student have a child of her own?
5. Is this student moving from place to place?
6. Was a step sheet provided for the student to finish the work?
7. How is the assignment relevant to the student's motivation?
8. Is the student given opportunities to work with other students?

STEPS	ACTION
1.	*Teach the whole class* time management and planning backward. For example, if an assignment is due on Friday, what day do students have to start working? In addition, have students plan what grades they intend to receive in each class.
2.	Talk to the student one-on-one if possible and communicate through "sticky notes."
3.	Assess the reasons for the work not being done.
4.	Ask for a plan from the student about when the work can be completed. Identify the smaller, in-between steps to get it done.
5.	Identify the consequences of work not being completed.

How do you handle the student who is inappropriately sexual (jokes, stories, gestures, etc.)?

STEPS	ACTION
1.	*Teach the whole class* (at least five minutes) about sexual-harassment laws, guidelines, and the seriousness of the law, particularly as it relates to required consequences at school and at work.
2.	Strictly forbid sexual harassment in your classroom.
3.	Document the specific behaviors/comments in writing.
4.	Refer the student to the administration.
5.	If a student sexually harasses others repeatedly, it may be an indicator of sexual abuse. In this case the student also needs to be referred to a counselor, nurse, administrator, etc.

How do you handle a bully?

Bullying is both a system issue and an individual issue. In organizational research, there is a phenomenon known as "isomorphism," which means that what happens at one level of the organization happens at least in some measure at all levels. So if you have student bullies, you also tend to have teacher bullies and administrator bullies. In most school systems, student bullying is a zero-tolerance activity.

STEPS	ACTION
1.	Identify the action or behavior that was unacceptable.
2.	Ask this question: "When you did that, what did you want or need?"
3.	Identify alternative behavior(s).
4.	Recommend/require that the bully get involved in some type of supervised community service.
5.	Refer the case to the administration.

How do you handle the instigator—the student who creates many of the problems?

It's important to understand how an instigator works. First of all, instigators love omissions, the part of the story that is not told. And the instigator almost always uses sexual innuendo and insult. This can be verbal or nonverbal. Nonverbal messages often are used because they allow the instigator to be "innocent." Instigators also use a divide-and-conquer strategy; in other words, I'll tell you one thing and tell the other person something else.

If you wish to identify who your campus instigators are, a simple tool is available. Give every teacher and administrator a disposable camera. When there's a fight, the staff members take pictures. Students scatter almost immediately. But usually the instigators are watching the fight, and they're in most of the pictures of the fight.

To end the behavior, the following steps often help.

STEPS	ACTION
1.	First, talk individually to the students. This is the key question: *"Were you there when they said/did that?"* Almost always they weren't present; it was reported back to them.
2.	Ask who told them. Typically they won't tell you—particularly if it's a school bully. So you can say: *"Did you have a vision?"* At that point they often will tell you the person's name.
3.	Repeat Steps 1 and 2 with the next person. You tend to get the same name(s). This is your instigator.
4.	Put the instigator between the two individuals and ask each of them to tell the other what the instigator told them. Very quickly they hear the omission.
5.	If you want to end the behavior of the instigator, the instigator must receive the same consequences as the individuals who got into trouble as a result of the instigation.

What do you do when a student cheats?

ASK YOURSELF …

What is the "payoff" for cheating?

- A passing grade
- Reduced anxiety about tests
- Less pressure from parents

STEPS	ACTION
1.	Document the activity.
2.	Give a zero.
3.	Sometimes teachers will give a test or alternative activity to find out what learning has occurred.
4.	Determine the intervention based on the reason(s) for cheating.

How do you handle a situation where you suspect that a student is being abused or when a student tells you about it?

STEPS	ACTION
1.	Say to the student *before he/she tells you anything* that you are required by law to report abuse.
2.	Refer him/her to someone in the larger support system who would have time and resources to help.
3.	Limit your personal involvement due to issues pertaining to both litigation and expertise.

What do you do about tardiness?

Tardiness is a system issue. A key issue in tardiness is prevention. What are the norms for your campus? Are students allowed to be tardy? What is the consequence of being tardy on your campus? When there is no campus system and the individual teacher must decide how to handle tardies, there will be a problem with students being tardy.

STEPS	ACTIONS
1.	What is the consequence on your campus for being tardy? Is that consequence enforced? If so, then follow campus policy.
2.	If the consequence is not enforced, then you must set up a classroom system for tardies.
OPTIONS	a) Give important information the first minute of class. b) Be at the door to greet students with a smile. c) Lock the door. Don't allow tardy students in for a few minutes. d) Give extra-credit points for students who arrive punctually; in other words, set up your own system of rewards for being in class on time.

How do you handle inappropriate language?

STEPS	ACTION
1.	Teach registers of language (see Appendix, page 139).
2.	Distinguish between a slip and habitual use.
3.	Ask the student to write five other ways to say it in formal register.
4.	Explain that language is a "hidden rule" of environments and being able to use the language of any environment is a key way of winning in that environment.
5.	Build a relationship of mutual respect with each student. Many times inappropriate language is a deliberate show of disrespect, often because there's no relationship.

How do you handle a personal threat?

1. What is this threat about?
2. Is it serious or simply said in anger?
3. Is it repeated?
4. Is the student using it to show his/her toughness to another student?
5. Is it gang-related?

STEPS	ACTION
1.	De-escalate the situation immediately, then ask yourself the above questions. *Do not show fear to the student.*
2.	Have a private conversation with the student and try to determine the cause of the threat and the intent of the threat.
3.	If you perceive it to be a serious threat, report it immediately to the administration and ask that the student be removed from your classroom.
4.	Document the incident in writing.
5.	Get an answering machine for your home phone and take personal precautions.

How do you handle a student who is openly disrespectful of you? How do you handle a student who seems to have no trust in or respect for adults?

Many beginning teachers believe that if they are nice to students, students will be nice to them in return. This is not the case. There must be mutual respect in the classroom. Mutual respect involves three things: *high expectations, insistence, and support.* Mutual respect is taught, it is earned, it is reciprocated, and it comes from insistence. Admittedly, it is hard for a beginning teacher to get a handle on this because in part it's earned and in part it stems from reputation.

STEPS	ACTION
1.	Do I have a relationship of mutual respect with this student? Is it possible to have one?
2.	Have I clearly explained my guidelines and expectations to the students? Write them down and have students copy them, sign them, and hand them in to you. Keep the signed papers on file so you can show a student that the guidelines were explained.
3.	Use the "Future Story" technique with the student (see Appendix, page 140).
4.	Teach the "hidden rules" of school so that the student is clear about what is needed.
5.	Call the student by name. Use "Please," "Thank you," and other courtesies with the student. You also may decide to call the student by "Mr." or "Ms." and their last name (this can make a huge difference), but don't do so sarcastically.

How do you handle a student who almost certainly is under the influence of drugs?

STEP	ACTION
1.	Immediately refer him/her to the office or the nurse. Just say, "I notice you aren't feeling well; you must leave the room." No exceptions. There may be serious health consequences for the student (death, coma, etc.). You also need to make sure you aren't potentially liable.

How do you deal with a student who makes sexual advances toward you, the teacher?

First, try all of the preventive strategies. If those don't work, then move on to the next steps.

	PREVENTIVE STRATEGIES
1.	***Never*** be in a room alone with ***any*** high school student, male or female, with the door closed.
2.	If a student asks for extra help, leave the door open. Work in clear view of the hallway, or work with a group of students.
3.	If a student compliments you, say, "Thank you." Go on to the lesson.
4.	If any students come to your home uninvited, do not let them in. Either don't answer the door, or tell them you will see them at school.
5.	Don't attend a student-sponsored party after school hours or on the weekend.
6.	***Never*** share any information about your private sexual life with students. To do so is to invite advances.
7.	Do ***not*** have favorite students. This invites advances as well.
8.	Do ***not*** wear sexually suggestive clothing (tight, revealing, etc.).

	STOPPING STRATEGIES
1.	Tell the student you appreciate the interest and compliments, but you are the teacher, not his/her buddy or friend. Therefore, the comments in class must stop.
2.	If the comments/actions do not stop, then the student must be referred to the office.
3.	In extreme cases the student is assigned to another teacher.

How do you handle an angry student?

Anger is almost always based upon fear. If you can find out the fear, you can address in part the anger. Rage, on the other hand, is almost always based on shame. Shame is much harder to identify because generally it isn't connected to a specific person.

STEPS	ACTION
1.	Isolate the student.
2.	Diffuse the anger by staying in the adult voice. Validate the student's feelings.
3.	Calm the student. One of the quickest ways is to have the student look at the ceiling. When eyes are up, the brain cannot access feelings. So have the student look up for a while.
4.	Try to find the cause of the anger. Was there a specific incident? Is it a person? Is it a prior incident before school? Is it a home issue? Is there a biochemical issue?
5.	Redirect the feelings from the personal to the issue.
6.	Refer the student to a counselor, nurse, administrator, etc.

Where do you draw the line between personal and professional involvement with students?

Some of the hardest parts of teaching are the emotional issues and trauma that you see unfolding before your eyes in the personal lives of students. Knowing where to draw the line of involvement is essential to your success. And the line is not always at the same place. Though there are principles, to be sure, it also depends on both the student and the situation.

First of all, when you attempt to solve students' problems, be aware that your help could actually play a role in making them a victim. You can teach them problem-solving skills and identify resources and questioning techniques. ***But your role is not to solve their problems.*** Your role is to link them to resources, identify the questions that need to be answered, provide problem-solving skills, help them access support systems, and help them get educated. All this is part and parcel of learning and growing, being a professional, and discovering how to set limits and boundaries.

STEPS	ACTION
1.	Ask yourself the questions on page 121. If it is life-or-death, refer it immediately to an administrator.
2.	*Do not give money or rides.*
3.	Back away from the situation and pretend you are sitting and watching this movie (story) they are telling you about. In other words, view the situation with healthy detachment. If you jumped into the movie, would it make any difference in the ending, or would it just complicate the story?
4.	What are the resources I can link the student to?

ASK YOURSELF ...

1. Is this a life-or-death situation?
2. Is there someone who could provide better resources and skills than I can?
3. Do I have enough expertise even to discuss this topic at all?
4. Which parts of this story are true? What has been omitted from this story?
5. Do I have the time, energy to be involved?
6. If I were involved, could I make any difference?
7. *Key question:* Does this individual really want this situation to be different? Does he/she get a payoff, or is he/she truly a victim?
8. Will my involvement make a difference in this individual's future story? Five years from now, will this involvement have impacted the student's life in a positive way?

How do you handle a frantic student whose parent requires him/her to get straight A's?

ASK YOURSELF …

1. What is the "payoff" for the parent?
2. Does the parent seem to have a need for bragging rights?
3. Does the parent see the child as proof of his/her ability to parent?
4. Does the parent see all A's as necessary for admittance to a certain college or university?
5. Does the parent have nothing else to do?

STEPS	ACTION
1.	Talk to the student and try to identify the payoff for the parent.
2.	Schedule a parent conference or call the parent.
3.	Describe the issues the student is experiencing and identify possible consequences of extreme pressure—health problems, drug use, dropping out, even suicide.
4.	Refer parent (discreetly) to other parents who have one or more children in college. Perfection is often an issue for parents of first-born children and for those who haven't had much exposure to adult children.
5.	Prepare a parent brochure or have a parent meeting where parents whose children went through your high school talk about their own children's experiences in college/university and how the high school and college experiences are different. Ask these parents to particularly identify the high school attitudes and skills that then translate over to college. Many high school parents (particularly with a first-born first child) have very little concept of college today.

VERBAL ABUSE

Verbal abuse occurs when the teacher or administrator is in the parent voice. It is the tone of sarcasm that makes it verbally abusive. It is designed to hurt, and it is subtle. If the oral repartee is two-way—in other words, if the student can equally engage in the repartee—it is not damaging. But if the exchange is one-way—in other words, I can say it to you, but you can't say anything back—then it is very damaging and creates a hostile, win-lose environment that builds latent hostility. Many teachers and administrators at the secondary level use verbal abuse as a control mechanism. However, it significantly reduces learning.

TYPE	DEFINITION	EXAMPLE
Threatening	To manipulate by threatening loss or pain	"Do that again, and I'll kick you out." "My mom's going to call you." "You'll flunk this class." "You mess with me, and my dad will get you."
Name calling	To call the other person names, including terms of endearment that are said sarcastically	"Well, darling …" "You're a bitch!" "You're a troublemaker!"
Forgetting	To forget incidents, promises, and agreements for the purpose of manipulation	"I don't know what you're talking about." "I never agreed to that!" "I never promised to behave."
Ordering	To give orders instead of asking respectfully	"Do your work and shut up." "Quit looking at me."
Denial	To deny the reality of the other person	"You made that up." "You're crazy." "Where did you get that?" "I never said that. I never did that."

TYPE	DEFINITION	EXAMPLE
Abusive anger	To use anger, both verbally and nonverbally in unpredictable outbursts to put the blame for his/her own inadequacies on the other person. It includes verbal rage, snapping at person, and shouting. It's part of the anger/addiction cycle in which the person releases inner tension. It can be triggered by changes at home or school, fears, the current sense of power, feelings of dependency or inadequacy, or unmet needs.	Teacher: "Why didn't the homework get done?" Student: "You're a bitch!" (gets up and stomps out of the room). Student: "I don't understand." Teacher: Throws down the pencil and yells, "You never understand! Why are you in this class anyway?"
Withholding	To remain cool and indifferent, to be silent and aloof, to reveal as little as possible	"What do you want me to say?" "Why should I care if you like it?" "I don't have to tell you how to do it." "I don't have to answer your question."
Countering	To express the opposite of what the person says	"This assignment is hard." "No, it's not. It's easy." "You're not fair." "Yes, I am."
Disguised as a joke	To make disparaging comments disguised as a joke	"You couldn't find your head if it wasn't attached." "You're so ugly, only your mother could love you." "When God was giving out brains, you thought he said trains, and you got in the wrong line!"

TYPE	DEFINITION	EXAMPLE
Blocking and diverting	To prevent the conversation from continuing, often by switching the topic	"You're just trying to have the last word." "You heard me. I shouldn't have to repeat myself." "That's a lot of crap!" "Did anybody ask you?" "Will you get off my back?"
Accusing and blaming	To blame the other person for one's own anger, irritation, or insecurity	"You're looking for trouble." "You're just trying to pick a fight." "You don't care about me."
Judging and criticizing	To judge and express the judgment in a negative, critical way; to judge a third person and express it in a negative, critical way	"You're stupid." "You're lazy." "You're an awful teacher." "She can't keep anything straight."
Trivializing	To diminish and make insignificant the work or contribution of the other person	"I know you helped me do the problem, but you should have given me the answer." "I realize you did the work yourself, but did you have to write your name that big?"

Adapted from Patricia Evans, *Verbally Abusive Relationships*

PROCEDURES CHECKLIST: GRADES 9–12

The following checklist for Grades 9–12 has been adapted from Guidelines for the First Days of School, from the Research Development Center for Teacher Education, Research on Classrooms, University of Texas, Austin.

Jennifer Ratka, Lancaster, New York, prepared this sample checklist.

STARTING CLASS	MY PROCEDURE
Taking attendance	While students work on the focus activity, I check by using the seating chart and jot down the date in the corner of the chart if a student is absent.
Marking absences	In addition to the computer program into which we're required to input attendance, I keep a notebook that is divided into five sections—one for each class. In this notebook, I note absences and any behavior issues that I discuss with students, as well as other incidents that I may wish to document.
Tardy students	Students who come late to class without a pass are assigned detention; there's a form that the students fill out. I simply hand the form to the student during class.
Giving makeup work for absentees	I have a hanging-file crate on my back table with a file for each class. If a student is absent, I write down the activities from the class, homework, and upcoming due dates, plus I attach handouts. I place this packet in the file folder standing up. Upon returning to class, the students know to check the absent file, then check with me if they have questions.
Enrolling new students	Teachers receive a drop/add form in their mailboxes. I will then gather important documents (i.e., course outline, student information sheet, and current reading and materials). I review the seating chart, find an appropriate place for him/her, introduce him/her to the class informally, and then will discuss after class the plan for making up the work we've covered so far.
Un-enrolling students	Students must have teachers sign a withdrawal form and a textbook-return form in order to drop a class.

STARTING CLASS	MY PROCEDURE
Students who have to leave school early	Students show the proper pass from the office at the start of class, then leave at the appointed time.
Warm-up activity (that students begin as soon as they walk into classroom)	Directions are written on the board for the focus activity. Students complete it in their notebooks/journals on a worksheet.

INSTRUCTIONAL TIME	MY PROCEDURE
Student movement within classroom	I state directions clearly and ask students to repeat directions or provide directions on a handout.
Use of cell phones and headphones	Headphones are to be in the student's locker. If a student enters class with them, I ask him/her to go put them in the locker—or else I hang onto them. Cell phones are not permitted during school hours. If a student has a cell phone out, I ask the student for it and place it on my desk until the end of class.
Going to restroom	Students have 15 passes per month in their school agenda (planner). A student may sign out a pass and ask for permission to use the restroom. Students are asked to wait until an appropriate time in the lesson.
Getting students' attention	At the beginning of class, I will start with a "Good morning" and remind students of what they're supposed to be working on (focus activity), and I will tell them how long they'll have to complete it. During group activities, I use a cooking timer that beeps, signaling the students' time is up. I then ask students to put their work/conversations on hold until I'm finished giving directions or going over information.
Students talking during class	If I am speaking or a student is speaking, I will ask the students who are talking among themselves to please stop and be engaged listeners—or say they may add their comments later. Or I ask them to repeat what was said last.

INSTRUCTIONAL TIME	MY PROCEDURE
What students do when their work is completed	Students are always given directions as to what they should do when their work is done. I have an agenda on a large easel. Options include reviewing vocabulary, reading free-read books, or starting the next activity.
Working together as group(s)	With some group activities, I assign roles, and students are responsible for completing the work designated to that role. Other times I ask all students to be active in taking notes, responding, listening, etc.
Handing in papers/homework	Many times I will have students turn in papers on the back table before starting the focus activity. Occasionally I'll ask students to have the work out on their desks while working on the focus activity and I'll go around to collect or check the work.
Appropriate headings for papers	For informal assignments, students need the date and their name on the top of the paper. Other assignments and projects sometimes require a title page with their name, my name, the date, title, and class section.
Bringing/distributing/ using textbooks	The class set of textbooks is on a shelf. If students need them for class, I will ask them to pick one up as part of the directions on the board before the focus activity. If students need to bring a book with them, I will remind them the class before and also put a sign in the doorway so students see it when they enter the room.
Leaving room for special class	Not applicable
Students who don't have paper and/or pencils	I have a crate on the back table with extra paper in it. I also have a cup with pens on the table. Students know that if they need these items they can get up and get one without bothering other students or the teacher.

INSTRUCTIONAL TIME	MY PROCEDURE
Signal(s) for getting student attention	At the beginning of class, I start with a "Good morning" and then tell students what to get started on (focus activity). During group activity I frequently use a timer. When the timer goes off, students know they need to stop their conversations and listen for the next set of directions. I wait until they're all done talking and looking at me. Sometimes students in the class will help with the process by adding, "Shhh … she's going to give us directions."
Touching other students in classroom	I introduce the rules to the students at the beginning of the school year. One rule is "Respect others," and I explain what this means and what it looks like. This rule includes keeping your hands to yourself. If a student is not following this rule, I will redirect him/her, then if this doesn't stop the behavior, I will give him/her a "behavior management referral," which then results in detention.
Laboratory procedures (materials and supplies, safety routines, cleaning up)	I have several bins of markers, a bin of scissors and glue sticks, and a box of magazines that students may use for various activities in the classroom. I store these bins on a shelf. Students are allowed to use them as long as they put them away properly. They're very good at putting supplies back after using them.
Students who get sick during class	If a student isn't feeling well, he/she may sign a pass to go to the health office. The nurse will call the room to let me know if the student will be staying there for a short time or returning to class.
Using pencil sharpener	Students may get up to use the pencil sharpener at any time during class. Most will wait until there's an appropriate time in the lesson.
Listing assignments/ homework/due dates	I use an easel with a pad of paper on it. The easel has the daily agenda on it, along with a list of homework and due dates. Students can flip back to the previous class if they want to check on anything.

INSTRUCTIONAL TIME	MY PROCEDURE
Systematically monitoring student learning during instruction	I frequently ask students the following kinds of questions: • "Does that make sense?" • "Everybody OK with that?" • "Any questions?" I also circulate frequently during group work, listening in on discussions and checking work. In addition, I ask a lot of questions to verify student understanding. I "scaffold" questions to include higher-order thinking skills in order to determine if students are fully grasping the subject matter.

ENDING CLASS	MY PROCEDURE
Putting things away	I give my students very precise instructions about where to put things when they're done. I also write the instructions on the board and sometimes will put them on a worksheet/group-activity direction sheet. If a student asks me, I'll ask him/her to check with a friend, then if he/she still doesn't understand to come and see me.
Dismissing class	Students aren't dismissed by the bell, they're dismissed by the teacher. I frequently include exit slips and/or a summarizing activity to end class, which usually takes us to the bell. Then I ask students to turn in the summarizing activity or hold onto it until the next class—and to have a nice afternoon.
Collecting papers and assignments	Most of the time I have students turn in papers on the back table. While they work on the focus activity, I check the papers to make sure all students have turned in the work. Sometimes I'll have the students pass their papers to the front while they're working on the focus activity.

OTHER	MY PROCEDURE
Lining up for lunch/recess/special events	Students line up quietly at the door, and the last student is expected to shut the door behind him/her.
Walking to lunch/recess	Not applicable
Putting away coats and backpacks	Students aren't allowed to have coats or backpacks with them during the school day. They must place these items in their lockers before classes start.
Cleaning out locker	In early June, 10 minutes are provided during the first block/period of the day for students to clean out their lockers. Janitors bring up large garbage cans, and members of Student Council circulate to accept any binders, folders, index cards, etc., that students want to donate rather than throw away.
Preparing for fire drills and/or bomb threats	During the first few classes I discuss with students the proper procedures and exit for any drills that take place. Once the alarm sounds, I remind students of where we're going and to move quickly and quietly. We all stay together. Teachers have a laminated sign with their last names on them. Teachers hold up the signs, students gather by their teacher, and the teachers take attendance.
Going to gym for assemblies/pep rallies	I remind students to quietly walk down the hall and that we'll all be sitting together. I sit with the students during the assembly in order to monitor behavior.
Respecting teacher's desk and storage areas	I have items that students may need (e.g., staplers, tape, extra pens, etc.) on the back table, and students are free to use those items at any time. This limits interruptions during class time.
Appropriately handling/using computers/equipment	Students must ask for permission to use the computer. Each student has his/her own "log in" to use. Students are allowed to use school e-mail, Internet browsers, and word-processing tools. I supervise students closely to make sure they're being appropriate; the web filter on school computers also helps with this matter.

STUDENT ACCOUNTABILITY	MY PROCEDURE
Late work	With block scheduling, I see my students only every other day. I'll accept work one day after it's due, with 10% taken off the score. If I don't have an assignment the following class, I have students stay after school to complete the assignment.
Missing work	If a student is missing an assignment because he/she was absent, I'll remind him/her and set a due date. I'll put this in writing and have the student sign it. If a student didn't complete an assignment, I'll have him/her stay after school with me to complete it. If he/she doesn't stay after school, I'll assign him/her detention and call home.
Extra credit	I offer extra-credit opportunities at various points throughout the semester. For example, if students read an extra book in their free time or find our vocabulary words in the newspaper, then I'll give them a few extra points on their lowest quiz grade.
Redoing work and/or retaking tests	I'll have students redo assignments, especially research papers, to bring up their grades and to make sure they understand the skills and process. Unless there are extenuating circumstances, I don't allow students to retake tests. If I do, then I always create an alternate version.
Incomplete work	Students will receive partial credit and be asked to "stay after" to complete the work. I'll give them some (not all) of the points back.
Neatness	Major assignments are word-processed; homework and in-class activities must be written legibly. If I can't read it, it's wrong: The student doesn't get credit.
Papers with no names	I rarely receive papers with no names. If I do, I'll return the papers, and then the one student will usually say, "I didn't get mine back"—and then I can remind him/her about putting his/her name on work in order to receive credit.

STUDENT ACCOUNTABILITY	MY PROCEDURE
Using pens, pencils, colored markers	Extra pens can be found in a cup on the back table for student use. I also have bins of markers that sometimes students need to use for group activities or for illustrating their vocabulary words. Students know where to find these supplies—and that returning them after use is expected.
Using computer-generated products	Not applicable
Internet access on computers	When we use computers, I usually have the sites bookmarked or links provided that students need to use. I reiterate our school's policy on appropriate use and remind them that they need to be on task. I usually have an extra set of printouts of pages from the Internet sources in case one or more students aren't using the computers appropriately.
Setting and assigning due dates	I set due dates that allow students to work effectively and seek extra help if needed. I tell students the due date when I assign the project.
Writing on back of paper	Most assignments are word-processed, so they're single-sided. Students may write on both sides of the paper.
Makeup work and amount of time for makeup work	Students have 10 days upon return to school to make up missed assignments/classwork. (This is school policy.)
Letting students know assignments missed during absence	Students are given a carbon copy (two-ply) "contract" that lists missed work and the due date. Students sign this form, return one copy to the teacher, and keep the other copy.
Percentage of grade for major tests, homework, etc.	• Tests are 50%. • Quizzes and projects are 30%. • Homework and classwork are 20%. My school requires that tests are 50% and that teachers administer at least two tests per quarter.

STUDENT ACCOUNTABILITY	MY PROCEDURE
Explaining your grading policy	I explain my grading policy to students at the beginning of the school year, and it's on the course outline. I also send home a letter to parents that students must return, signed, that explains the policy. I reiterate it to parents at Open House. I also provide students with progress reports every five weeks so they know where they stand. They're required to have their parents sign these progress reports as well.
Letting new students know your procedures	All policies and procedures are explained on the first day of school. The first week sets the tone, and students catch on to the routines very quickly.
Having contact with all students at least once during week	I greet students at the door and say hi or ask how they're doing. This ensures that I have some personal interaction with all students. By being in the hallway, I also can greet students who may have been absent, thereby checking in with them as well.
Exchanging papers	If I have students correct something in class, I have them switch and switch again. We then go over the answers. Depending on the assignment, I may collect it to verify and record. Otherwise, students pass them back to one another, and we discuss areas of concern.
Using Internet for posting assignments and sending them in	Teachers can have a website through the school district's website. Some teachers use the website to post notes, homework, and related course information. I have had students e-mail me papers when their computer printers ran out of ink.

HOW WILL YOU ...	MY PLAN
Determine grades on report cards (components and weights of those components)?	There are four quarters and a final exam. Each quarter and the final exam comprise 20% of the final grade. As noted above, for each marking period tests are worth 50%, quizzes and projects count 30%, and homework and classwork are worth 20%. I always have at least 25 grades per quarter.
Grade daily assignments?	I determine the amount of points I want the assignment to be worth, depending on time, difficulty, etc. I then break down the assignment into the main points/items I'll be looking for, then determine how much I want each point to be worth.
Record grades so that assignments and dates are included?	In addition to the computer gradebook we're required to use, I keep a "hard copy" (paper) gradebook. I record the dates that assignments are collected in the paper gradebook. I also keep a binder that has all my handouts and lesson plans. On each handout, in the top-right-hand corner, I write down the date assigned and the date turned in.
Have students keep records of their own grades?	Students keep papers in their notebooks. For major writing assignments, they keep a running log in a writing portfolio that I store in my classroom.
Make sure your assignments and grading reflect progress against standards?	"Scaffold" assignments to reflect the skills and processes they are expected to attain based on the standards. I also develop and use rubrics based on the main topics in each of the standards.
Notify parents when students are not passing or having other academic problems?	I make frequent phone calls and also keep guidance counselors updated. I send home five-week reports with the students to have their parents sign. If it doesn't come back signed, regardless of the grade, I call home.
Contact parents if problem arises regarding student behavior?	I call home immediately and document the date, time, and a brief description of the conversation.

HOW WILL YOU …	MY PLAN
Contact parents with positive feedback about their child?	I try to make at least one phone call per week to congratulate different parents on their son's or daughter's achievement. Once a quarter I send home a note/card to at least three students.
Keep records and documentation of student behavior?	I have a binder that is divided into sections for each class. Behind the divider I include the information sheet that I have students fill out at the start of the school year; any detention forms or behavior-management referrals; and a log that lists conversations with parents, administrators, and guidance counselors.
Document adherence to IEP (individualized education plan)?	I keep the special education/resource room teachers updated on everything we're doing in the classroom, along with upcoming important dates. For other concerns, such as preferred seating, I make sure the student has a seat near the front and center of the room. For testing accommodations, I let the special education teachers know when there will be a test or in-class writing assignment. The teacher will then discuss it with the student to decide if he/she will take it in class or in an alternate location.
Return graded papers in timely manner?	I work hard to return papers, with comments, within a week. Longer papers (research/thesis papers) often take two or three weeks.
Monitor students who have serious health issues (peanut allergies, diabetes, epilepsy, etc.)?	Teachers receive a list at the beginning of the school year about students with health issues. I review the list and make sure students are comfortable discussing any needs with me. For example, if a student needs to drink fluids or have his/her pulse checked, I make sure to tell him/her privately at the beginning of the year that he/she may leave class if needed. For food allergies, I'm careful about any snacks/treats I bring into the classroom.

APPENDIX

VOICES

CHILD

- **Quit picking on me.**
- **You don't love me.**
- **You want me to leave.**
- **Nobody likes (loves) me.**
- **I hate you.**
- **You're ugly.**
- **You make me sick.**
- **It's your fault.**
- **Don't blame me.**
- **She/he did it.**
- **You make me mad.**
- **You made me do it.**

PARENT

- **You shouldn't (should) do that.**
- **It's wrong (right) to do __________.**
- **That's stupid, immature, out of line, ridiculous.**
- **Life's not fair. Get busy.**
- **You are good, bad, worthless, beautiful (any judgmental, evaluative comment).**
- **You do as I say. If you weren't so __________, this wouldn't happen to you.**
- **Why can't you be like __________?**

ADULT

- **In what ways could this be resolved?**
- **What factors will be used to determine the effectiveness, quality, of __________?**
- **I would like to recommend __________.**
- **What are choices in this situation?**
- **I am comfortable (uncomfortable) with __________.**
- **Options that could be considered are __________.**
- **For me to be comfortable, I need the following things to occur: __________.**
- **These are the consequences of that choice/action: __________.**
- **We agree to disagree.**

Adapted from work of Eric Berne, *Games People Play*

REGISTERS OF LANGUAGE

REGISTER	EXPLANATION
FROZEN	Language that is always the same. For example: Lord's Prayer, wedding vows, etc.
FORMAL	The standard sentence syntax and word choice of work and school. Has complete sentences and specific word choice.
CONSULTATIVE	Formal register when used in conversation. Discourse pattern not quite as direct as formal register.
CASUAL	Language between friends characterized by a 400- to 800-word vocabulary. Word choice general and not specific. Conversation dependent upon nonverbal assists. Sentence syntax often incomplete.
INTIMATE	Language between lovers or twins. Language of sexual harassment.

Adapted from Martin Joos' research by Ruby K. Payne, *A Framework for Understanding Poverty*

FUTURE STORY

1. Draw 20 circles on a piece of paper and one circle in the front of the 20 circles. (See drawing on page 141.)

2. You say this to the student:

3. Let me tell you how our classroom looks through the eyes of a teacher. Here is what the teacher sees that you do not see. [Put an x on a circle and say …] This student here: His father is dying, and he goes home at night and takes care of his father all night while his mother works. [Put an x on another circle and say …] This student here: She just found out she is pregnant and doesn't know what to do. [Put an x on another circle and say …] This girl is in love with this girl over here (another circle), but that girl is in love with this boy (another x). This student here (another x) is supposed to go to Harvard, and she has to have perfect scores on everything or she's in trouble at home. This student here (x): If I call home and tell her mother that she doesn't have her homework, her mother sits down and helps her. But this student here (x): If I call home and tell his mother he doesn't have his homework, his father beats him. So I can call the parent of this student but not this one.

4. And do you know what they all want from me? They want me to be ***fair.*** And I ask you: How will I do that? [At this point in time, the student usually doesn't know what to say.]

5. Draw the rectangle (page 142) with the two teams and two goals and give the student one minute to tell you the rules of football, basketball, or soccer. Then you ask the student … How do you play the game if there are no goals? The student will usually make an attempt or two using the rules with a goal. Finally he or she will say something like: I guess you just run around and fight with each other. You say to the student … Isn't that what you are doing?

6. Then you ask the students to make lists of goals for themselves. You explain that the classroom will never be fair unless you use it to help you reach your own goals.

7. You meet with the student every two weeks to monitor the progress toward his/her goals.

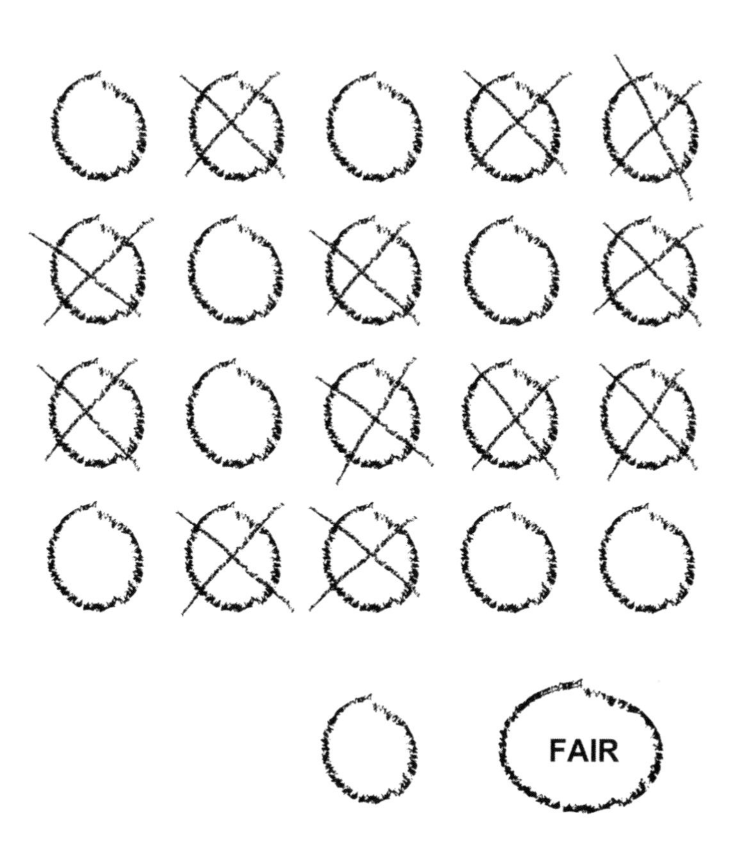

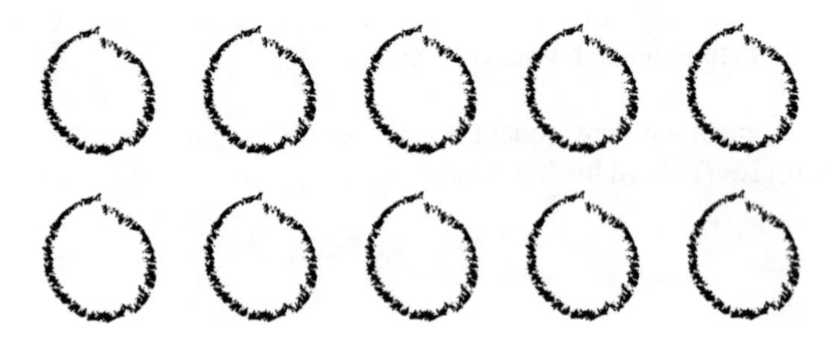

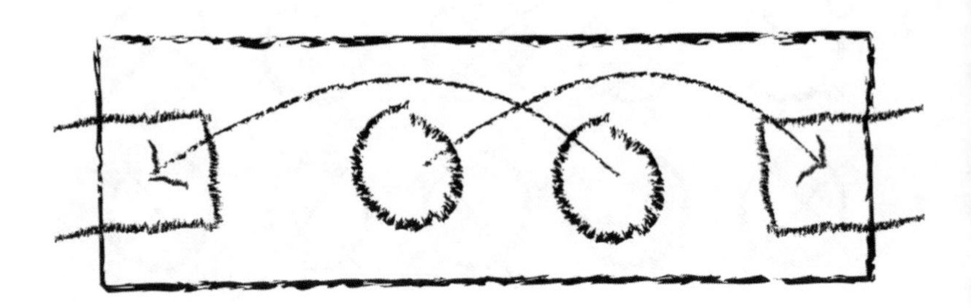

www.ahaprocess.com

aha! Process, Inc.
P.O. Box 727
Highlands, TX 77562
(800) 424-9484
Fax: (281) 426-5600
store@ahaprocess.com

Want your own copies? Want to give a copy to a friend? Please send:

______ COPY/COPIES of *Working with Students: Discipline Strategies for the Classroom*

BOOKS: $10.00/each + $4.50 first book plus $2.00 for each additional book, shipping/handling

MAIL TO:

NAME ______________________________

ORGANIZATION ______________________________

ADDRESS ______________________________

____

PHONE(S) ______________________________

E-MAIL ADDRESS(ES) ______________________________

____

METHOD OF PAYMENT:

PURCHASE ORDER # ______________
Please submit signed copy of purchase order with completed order form.

CREDIT CARD TYPE ______________ EXP ______

CREDIT CARD # ______________

CHECK $ ________ CHECK # ________

SUBTOTAL $ ______

SHIPPING $ ______

SALES TAX $ ______ 6.25% IN TEXAS

TOTAL $ ______

eye-opening
aha!
learning

More eye-openers at ... www.ahaprocess.com

- **If you are interested in more information regarding seminars or training, we invite you to visit our website at www.ahaprocess.com**

- **Join our aha! Process News List!**
  Receive the latest income and poverty statistics ***free*** when you join! Then receive periodic news and updates, recent articles written by Dr. Payne, and more!

- **Register for Dr. Payne's U.S. National Tour**

- **Contact us to learn how you can apply the "Payne Model" to make systemic changes in your organization**

- **Visit our online store**
  - Books
  - Videos
  - Workshops

- **Additional programs/video series offered by aha! Process, Inc. include:**
  - *A Framework for Understanding Poverty*
  - *Meeting Standards & Raising Test Scores—When You Don't Have Much Time or Money*
  - *Tucker Signing Strategies for Reading*

- **For a complete listing of products, please visit www.ahaprocess.com**

who did read it liked it," he said in the dark, and kneeled above her, near her face.

"Wait," she said, and dunked her cigarette with a sizzle. Something like a wet smoke ring encircled him; tightened, loosened. What beasts we all are. What pigs, Thelma would say. *I love your shit.*

Bea found him a typist—Mae, a thirty-year-old black woman with an IBM Selectric in a little ranch house the color of faded raspberries on Shady Lane; there was a green parakeet in a cage and a small brown child hiding behind every piece of furniture. Bech was afraid Mae wouldn't be able to spell, but as it turned out she was all precision and copyediting punctilio; she was in rebellion against her racial stereotype, like a Chinese rowdy or an Arab who hates to haggle. It was frightening, seeing his sloppily battered-out, confusingly revised manuscript go off and come back the next weekend as stacks of crisp prim typescript, with a carbon on onionskin and a separate pink sheet of queried corrigenda. He was being edged closer to the dread plunge of publication, as when, younger, he would mount in a line of shivering wet children to the top of the great water slide at Coney Island—a shaky little platform a mile above turquoise depths that still churned after swallowing their last victim—and the child behind him would nudge the backs of his legs, when all Bech wanted was to stand there a while and think about it.

"Maybe," he said to Bea, "since Mae is such a whiz, and must need the money—you never see a husband around the place, just that parakeet—I should go over it once more and have her retype."

"Don't you dare," Bea said.

"But you've said yourself, you loathe the book. Maybe I can soften it. Take out that place where the video crew masturbates all over Olive's drugged body, put in a scene where they all come up to Ossining and admire the fall foliage." Autumn had invaded their little woods with its usual glorious depredations. Bech had begun to work in his insulated room two springs ago. Spring, summer, fall, winter, spring, summer, fall: those were the seven seasons he had labored, while little Donald turned twelve and Ann, so Judy had tattled, lost her virginity.

"I loathe it, but it's you," Bea said. "Show it to your publisher."

This was most frightening. Fifteen years had passed since he had submitted a manuscript to The Vellum Press. In this interval the company had been sold to a supermarket chain who had peddled it to an oil company who had in turn, not liking the patrician red of Vellum's bottom line, managed to foist the firm off on a West Coast lumber-and-shale-based conglomerate underwritten, it was rumored, by a sinister liaison of Japanese and Saudi money. It was like being a fallen woman in the old days: once you sold yourself, you were never your own again. But at each change of ownership, Bech's books, *outré* enough to reassure the public that artistic concerns had not been wholly abandoned, were reissued in a new paperback format. His long-time editor at Vellum, dapper, sensitive Ned Clavell, had succumbed to well-earned cirrhosis of the liver and gone to that three-martini luncheon in the sky. Big Billy Vanderhaven, who had founded the firm as a rich man's plaything in the days of the trifling tax bite and who had concocted its name loosely out of his own, had long since retired to Hawaii, where he lived with his fifth wife on a diet of seaweed and macadamia nuts. A great fadster, who had raced at Le Mans and mountain-climbed in Nepal and scuba-dived off Acapulco, "Big" Billy—so called sixty years ago to distinguish him from his effete and once socially prominent cousin, "Little" Billy Vanderhaven—had apparently cracked the secret of eternal life, which is Do Whatever You Please. Yet, had the octogenarian returned under the sponsorship of that Japanese and Saudi money to take the helm of Vellum again, the effect could have been scarcely less sensational than Henry Bech turning up with a new manuscript. Bech no longer knew the name of anyone at the firm except the woman who handled permissions and sent him his little checks and courtesy copies of relevant anthologies, with their waxen covers and atrocious typos. When at last, gulping and sitting down and shutting his eyes and preparing to slide, he dialled Vellum's number, it was the editor-in-chief he asked for. He was connected to the snotty voice of a boy.

"You're the editor-in-chief?" he asked incredulously.

"No I am not," the voice said, through its nose. "This is her secretary."

"Oh. Well could I talk to her?"

"May I ask who is calling, please?"

Bech told him.

"Could you spell that, please?"

"Like the beer but with an 'h' on the end like in 'Heineken.' "

"Truly? Well aren't we boozy this morning!"

There was a cascade of electronic peeping, a cup-shaped silence, and then a deep female voice saying, "Mr. Schlitzeh?"

"No, no. Bech. B-E-C-H. Henry. I'm one of your authors."

"You sure are. Absolutely. It's an honor and a pleasure to hear your voice. I first read you in Irvington High School; they assigned *Travel Light* to the accelerated track. It knocked me for a loop. And it's stayed with me. Not to mention those others. What can I do for you, sir? I'm Doreen Pease, by the way. Sorry we've never met."

From all this Bech gathered that he was something of a musty legend in the halls of Vellum, and that nevertheless here was a busy woman with her own gravity and attested velocity and displacement value. He should come to the point. "I'm sorry, too," he began.

"I *wish* we could get you in here for lunch some time. I'd love to get your slant on the new format we've given your reprints. We're just crazy about what this new designer has done, she's *just* out of the Rhode Island School of Design, but those stick figures against those electric colors, with the sateen finish, and the counterstamped embossing—"

"Stunning," Bech agreed.

"You know, it gives a *un*ity; for me it gives the shopper a handle on what *you* are all about, you as opposed to each individual title. The salesmen report that the chains have been really enthusiastic: some of them have given us a week in the window. And that ain't just hay, for quality softcover."